TRIBES
OF LIGHT

A Roadmap to Your Guides

ADRIENNE NIKKI COBB

SPELLBOUND

TRIBES OF LIGHT

A Roadmap to Your Guides

Copyright ©2022 by Adrienne Nikki Cobb

All rights reserved.

ISBN: 979-8-9853523-0-6 (Paperback)

ISBN: 979-8-9853523-1-3 (ebook)

Library of Congress Control Number: 2021925294

Printed in the United States of America

In love, adoration, and gratitude to
The Great Central Sun Angels and Jill Cassandra Baker
"1968—eternity"

"Our message to you is to know that you are loved beyond measure. We are here to awaken within your soul the remembrance that YOU are a Divine Being capable of wondrous endeavors that can enlighten the hearts of humankind into its higher purpose. You are never alone in the journey of life, but rather are always enfolded in the loving embrace of your Tribes of light who are eternally shining upon you like a thousand golden suns singing the praise of your living glory!

— Message from the Great Central Sun Angels

CONTENTS

LIFE CHANGING MEDITATION

Who are you?

You are an Infinite Being.

You have one hundred percent awareness.

You have Free Will.

You are a Multidimensional Being capable of infinite great and mighty things!

You are a Being of Unconditional Love—really feel that one, breathe it in. Say it out loud with me, "I Am a Being of Unconditional Love." It's like light medicine for every cell in your body.

Remembering these Universal truths will cause an instantaneous awakening in your DNA to turn on the switch for your unique super powers and the questing of your Soul Blueprint.

I'd like to you share with you a meditation that will assist you in Blessing YOU and Being the blessing you are to all of life.

This meditation acts as a living instrument of light to "qualify" or bless your energy and consciousness, to remember the Universal Truths above.

You're ready now, at this very moment to know yourself, to empower yourself, to free yourself! Let's get started....

Universal Principal; *We are all energy, before we are matter.*

You are affecting the energetic space around you with your actions, words, thoughts, feelings, intentions, unconscious, and nervous system all the time and it is affecting you.

Knowing you are spirit before you are matter super charges your Blessings, prayers and intentions because you now remember you are a powerful Infinite, Aware Being with Free Will and you are directing the energy of the Universe with your Intentions.

For instance, if you were going to take a trip or go into a meeting, then you'd bless your experience with whatever you intuitively feel would be good for you such as: clarity, healing, good weather, peaceful interactions, and a synchronicity of miracles or harmonious perfection for the highest good of all.

When you do this, you are programming your subconscious thoughts, emotions, and the world around you with your intention (mental vision), desire (heart feeling) and will (spiritual intention) to bless your day.

It sends out a clear message to the Universe what you wish to experience. In effect, you're telling the Universe to respond to you in this intended way. You'll find that doing this will interrupt negative tapes from your past, replacing them with new magical experiences.

We are like human batteries. When we connect to Source Energy, we charge our energy and body. When we ground it to the heart of the Planet, we create a healthy circuitry. Then we bring the energy up to our heart, which is the battery that supports both frequencies of energy.

This meditation will not only help you become congruent and aligned with what you want to manifest in your day but it will also raise your vibrational resonance and ignite your Soul Blueprint, while expanding you to be a living blessing to all of life in the process. This is a win/win/win, a triple bottom line for your life!

I do this meditation every morning and evening. It's a combination of a heart breathing meditation from Heartmath.org to center yourself and create coherence between your head and heart. This breathing technique reduces stress and anxiety in your body, mind and heart.

The other part of the meditation I learned from Christie Marie Sheldon in her Love or Above workshop. You can find her at www.christiesheldon.com

Morning and Evening Meditation

First, breathe into your heart for the count of five seconds, hold for five seconds, and breath out for ten seconds while focusing on gratitude for your life, your day, your home, your loved ones, etc. If you do this ten time's it's about three minutes to get your head and heart into coherence which opens you up to receive more light, transmissions, downloads, miracles and love or above energy.

Now, focus your awareness three hundred feet above your head to a portal of light that connects you to Source Energy.

Command the Cosmic Flow of Pure Love and Light down, in, around, and through you. Balancing and harmonizing, cleansing and rejuvenating your entire body and energy. Being it through all your chakras filling them with Pure Love and Light.

Then send this energy to the heart of the Planet. Connect your energy to a place that feels good, peaceful, abundant, and supportive for you.

Next, draw this energy back up through the bottoms of your feet, knees, hips, and into your heart.

Expand this energy around your body in a three hundred and sixty degree radius of light. Then send it out all the way around the Planet as a living blessing to all of life.

Open your heart in a circuitry to receive with gratitude Love or Above energy, a synchronicity of miracle, golden opportunities, and really good things coming your way throughout the day and while you sleep raising your vibrational resonance to its highest level possible in all ways in your life.

Hold your hands out in front of you like your holding a basketball. Fill this ball with Pure Love and Light three times by saying: This is a blessing ball for my day and my life.

Really feel love flooding into this ball of light from your heart center.

Say out loud or to yourself: I'm filling it with Pure Love and Light, Pure Love and Light, Pure Love and Light! Purified Source Energy, Purified Source Energy, Purified Source Energy!

Now add Grace and Gratitude. Grace quickens all your blessings and Gratitude opens your heart to receive it.

Say silently or out loud what you want to put into your Blessing Ball:

All problems are instantly resolved with harmonious perfection,

All my needs and desires are met even before I know what I need,

My body is happy and healed, vibrant,

I'm blessing my kids, pets, partner, family, friends, job, Earth, home with Pure Love and Light, I have the perfect partnership that matches my true self energy,

I'm putting in my Blessing Ball kindness, compassion, joy, equanimity in my relationship with myself and others. Forgiveness with any relationship problem.

that as soon as anyone is aware of me or thinks of me they are instantly blessed in Pure Love and Light.

Empowerment, unconditional love, strength, focus, clarity,

My bank accounts are overflowing with hundreds of thousands of dollars, unlimited fulfillment, success, abundance, peace, Love and Above Energy, blessings, miracles.

I'm asking my Tribes of Light, guides, angels and Source Energy to put anything that serves my highest good in my Blessing Ball. etc.

Get creative and listen to your heart's wisdom.

Next, breathe your Blessing Ball into your heart and radiate it out like a great golden sun all around the Earth to magnetize what you put in your Blessing Ball with Love and Above energy.

Practice: Always Staying Connected.

This will automatically ignite your Soul Blueprint and raise your Vibrational Resonance to your Highest Vibration.

WE LIVE WORLDS
WITHIN WORLDS

What does it mean? *"We live worlds within worlds."*

We are connected to other dimensions of consciousness all the time without having to go into meditation to be aware of them.

For instance, when you're walking through the woods, your passing by fairies, tree spirits, devas, animals, and many more nature beings all around you whether you're aware of it or not consciously. We are coexisting in this world together. Some people and children see them and are consciously aware of them.

When we go to churches, monasteries, or sacred power spots on the Earth we cross thresholds into the realms of angels, master teachers, and star portals.

Other examples of coexisting are:

- As we drive down freeways or sit in hospitals, Angels hover over us constantly, bringing answers to our prayers, guiding, and comforting us.

- Star Beings dwell among us as indigenous tribes, dolphins, and indigo children, bringing visions of the future.

- Planetary Beings act as diplomats in the United Nations and other organizations that encourage a peaceful society.

- Galactic Beings act in compassionate ways to inspire change in the world.

- Cosmic Beings bring forth transmissions and downloads of higher consciousness to shape the face of human evolution.

- On your sacred journey through these worlds upon worlds, you will have the opportunity to meet your Tribe of Light and ignite your Soul Blueprint DNA.

- You will also be given spiritual formulas to open your inner vision and access your life purpose. By learning how to trust your intuition and the feelings of your heart's wisdom you can access the greatest gifts of innate brilliance.

TRUSTING YOUR INTUITION

Your Inner Guidance System is an invaluable tool in the fulfillment of your Soul Blueprint. It allows you to be guided from a Higher Power that knows the very essence of your being, your soul attributes, what brings you fulfillment, love, and peace.

If we stayed connected with our intuition it would guide us in unimaginable ways of living an unlimited life.

We are all born with the gift of intuition built into us. Intuition is the language of our energy body. The other five physical senses are the language of the physical body. We are lucky to have two communication systems in our consciousness: one for the inner world and one for our outer world, and both of these systems are interrelated to one another.

We are all using our intuition all the time to survive, thrive, and coexist in this world.

The five senses we usually think of in our physical body are vision, hearing, taste, smell and touch.

Equally, there are ten Clair senses in our psychic or energetic body we use to move through the world as well.

If you're an Indigo child or adult, you were born with heightened gifts of intuition already fully developed. You are likely empathic, intuitive, and a high impath. You may also have special traits including the ability to use your intuitive skills to help others.

Here's an excellent article I came across from Emily Matweow, a gifted intuitive. If you're interested in a session with her, you can go to her website: www.emilymatweow.com.

'Meet the Clairs' – 10 Kinds of Intuition

Clair is a word describing types of clear sensitivity corresponding to our physical and intuitive senses. Clair begins words that name our intuitive abilities.

The following are definitions of the various Clair Senses:

Energy medicine writer and instructor Emily Matweow has identified ten Clairs that give shape to the different perspectives and talents of intuitive people:

- Clairvoyance: Intuitive Vision

- Clairaudience: Intuitive Audio or Hearing

- Clairsentience: Intuitive Knowing by Feeling

- Clairsalience: Intuitive Smell

- Clairtangency: Intuitive Knowing by Touching (psychometry)

- Clairtaction: Intuitive Touch (ethereal)

- Clairgustance: Intuitive Taste

- Clairempathy: Intuitive Feeling of Emotion

- Claireloquence: Intuitive Communicating

- Clairessence: Intuitive Embodiment

Claircognizance – Intuitive Knowledge

Clear knowledge is when a person has psychic knowledge without any physical explanation or reason. Claircognizance includes precognition and retro cognition – knowledge of the future and knowledge of the past. There are no restrictions as to what may be known with clear knowledge.

Clairvoyance – Intuitive Vision

The ability to see objects, actions, or events distant from the present without the use of eyes is called clairvoyance. It transcends time and space and may be a result of what is seen through the third eye (sometimes referred to as our mind's eye) or the fourth eye.

Clairaudience – Intuitive Audio or Hearing

This is the ability to perceive sounds or words and extrasensory noise from sources broadcasting from the spiritual or ethereal realm.

These tones exist beyond the reach of rational human experience and beyond the limitations of ordinary space and time. For example:

- sounds made by a person's body
- sounds made by living things
- sounds made by nature
- sounds made by man-made things
- sounds made by interactions of the above
- ethereal sounds like voices of the dead, specters, or mystic music

Clairsentience – Intuitive Knowing by Feeling

This refers to an ability to acquire knowledge by feeling. A person who feels the vibration of other people, animals, and places is clairsentient. There are many degrees of clairsentience, ranging from the perception of thoughts and emotions in others to their illnesses and injuries. This ability differs from clairvoyance because the knowledge comes only from feeling in the body.

Clairsentience includes an individual feeling the physical and emotional pain of land where atrocities have happened; jealousy, insecurity, fear, or displeasure in others; or others' physical pain.

Clairsalience – Intuitive Smell

Clairsalience, also known as clairscent or clairscentency, involves smelling a fragrance or odor of a substance, person, place, or animal not in one's surroundings. These odors are perceived without the use of the physical nose and beyond the limitations of ordinary time and space.

Clairtangency Intuitive Knowing by Touching

Clairtangency is psychometry. The clairtangent handles an object or touches something and in doing so knows information about the object or its owner or its history that was not known beforehand. Clairtangency can also apply to touching a living being.

Clairtaction – Intuitive Touch

I introduce this label for a "new" unnamed Clair. I chose taction because it is an archaic word defined as "the act of touching or making contact."

Clairtaction is the ability to sense being touched by a spiritual being or entity and the knowing of information about that spirit. Further, it includes a telekinetic-like ability to extend a touch to both physical and etheric entities in such a way that both the recipient and the psychic have awareness of the feeling. This means that the clairtactient may touch a person who is present or remote without physically touching him or her and the person being touched will, if aware enough, be able to identify where he or she is being touched and the nature of the touch. It also means that the clairtactient can touch something ethereal with both purpose and awareness.

Clairgustance – Intuitive Taste

Clear tasting involves being able to taste something without actually putting it into your mouth. It's the perfect diet plan.

Clairempathy – Intuitive Feeling of Emotion

Clairempathy is the ability to know people and their energies. A person who has clairempathy psychically experiences the thoughts or attitudes of a person, place, or animal and then feels the associated mental, emotional, physical, and/or spiritual results. The result of this clear empathetic experience may be a very physical response for the psychic in proportion to the psychic's empathic sensitivity.

Claireloquence – Intuitive Communicating

Claireloquence is another new Clair. It is the requirement to use precisely the right word or combination of words in order to accomplish a specific objective. Claireloquence connotes that it is the exact meaning of a word that is the result when it may in fact be the performative nature of the word or the exact phonology, or sound system, of the word to encode meaning that is the desired result. I believe that it can be either and both.

Clairessence – Intuitive Embodiment

Clairessence is a third new Clair. It is the fundamental "Clair of all Clairs." It is both the easiest and the most difficult to explain, for it is the Clair of Ascension; by the time we fully understand this Clair it will no longer be significant because we will be "it."

The origin of clairessence is the point of origin of our nature. It is the mathematical and vibrational perfection with which all life was created. It is the ideal we seek to attain in the successful embodiment and integration of all of our senses within our rational and non-rational selves. It is the state we seek to return to — a state without distortion that is more refined, by virtue of experience, than when it was created.

Intuitives Do It… With Clairity.

You can read through this list and notice, feel or sense which intuition feels most natural to you. The one you lean into most in a day without even thinking about it. Remember, you have most likely developed this form of your intuition over lifetimes.

Meet the Empath Styles

Along with the ten forms of clair-intuition see if you relate to these forms of empathy as well:

- **Emotional Empath**: picking up on the emotions/feelings of others.

- **Mental Empath**: picking up on the thoughts of others.

- **Physical Empath:** picking up on the physical symptoms/pain of others.

- **Animal/Plant/Nature Empath:** picking up on the wellbeing of plants, animals, land, Earth.

- **Global empath**: picking up on the collective consciousness.

The key to working with intuition, is it trust our feelings and our body wisdom. It's good to be aware of what levels of consciousness you are sensitive to.

If you feel overwhelmed by your empathy or intuition, I recommend you do the energy technique described below. This will help you stay connected to Spirit and balanced all throughout the day as you get stronger in your energy to be able to hold your own with the world around you.

CENTERING ENERGY TECHNIQUE

Begin by focusing your consciousness three hundred feet above your head where there is a portal of Light, Source Energy.

Call it forth, amplify it through your body to connect and clear your energy field with Pure Love & Light as it flows in around and through you.

Then send your energy to the core of the planet to ground this energy into the Earth.

Then bring the Source energy and Planetary energy back up again through the bottoms of your feet, knees, hips, and into your heart.

Expand this energy around you like a central sun in a three hundred and sixty degrees radius of light around your body, then send this energy out around the whole planet to be blessed in Pure Love and Light.

This technique will connect you to the highest Source beyond your or others influence of thoughts, emotions, projections, and judgements.

Allow this energy to clear your space. Breathe it in and out to super charge your energy with Pure Love and Light.

When you feel centered, neutral, grounded, then ask for guidance. You can get connected this way instantly or within a few minutes. *Trust your guidance.*

Although you may lean in to one form of intuition more than the others, the goal is to start being aware of all of them and asking your soul/higher self to turn on and connect all of them for you to use. It's very fulfilling to be that awake, alive, and tuned in to life. Your wisdom will be fully functioning in parts of your brain and awareness that have not been awakened before.

Your intuition is one of the first ways you begin to understand how multidimensional you really are by being sensitive to energy on a subtle level that is not always known by our five physical senses.

The worlds that we are overlapping with are dimensional. They are energetic like fairies or angels, but they definitely exist just as we do.

YOU'RE A
MULTIDIMENSIONAL BEING

Your energy governs your experience. You could have two totally different experiences if you were coming from your Higher Self or if you were coming from your unconscious self.

Our ability to experience our self in the reflection of this world, comes from what part of our consciousness we're focused on in the moment. Most of the time we are unconsciously hanging out in the perception of our inner child, ego, or unconscious self.

When we're looking at the world through the filter of our inner child, we will act like our inner child no matter our age. When we're at the world through the lens of our Higher Self, we will act like our Higher Self no matter our age.

At any time, you can shift your conscious awareness. The key is knowing how to access your different levels of consciousness for the type of experience you wish to have.

When you can shift to higher states of consciousness instead of hanging out in your lower states of consciousness you'll have a better attitude and have a better time.

Most people aren't even aware they are multidimensional and have the freedom to shift gears when they want to upgrade their life experience. It's similar to shifting states of mind or shifting emotional states of being.

The different states of being-ness are referred to as the inner child, the unconscious, the conscious mind, and the higher consciousness.

We tend to hang out in the lower states of consciousness by default. That is, we default to an automatic pilot state that was created in childhood.

The higher states of consciousness have their own levels and functions. They tie into your unique intuitive style.

- Heart intuition people tend to like being present in the soul body or they can get stuck in the lower emotional body.

- Mental intuition people like being present in the Higher Self or they can get stuck in lower ego body and denialism, control issues.

- Energetically intuition people tend to like being present in the Light Body or they can burn out with ADD/ADHD and other energetic intense issues and resistance to life.

- Spiritual intuition people tend to like being present in the I Am Presence or they can get stuck in their ego and arrogance, and the need to be right.

- Higher spiritual intuition people like being present in their Cosmic Presence or they can get stuck in their ego and aloofness to life.

Your Tribes of Light are connected with you at all times regardless of which level of consciousness your residing in. However, when your resonating with your higher states of consciousness, you can become aware of your Tribes of Light more easily and receive their guidance and support.

When you understand how to access these levels of consciousness, it can make traveling with the Tribes of Light more graceful and fun.

There are seven Tribes of Light that overlight and work with humanity. They are Cosmic Avatars, Galactic Councils, Planetary Light Beings, Star Tribes, Angelic Beings, Ascended Masters and Nature Spirits. They are your Tribe, Family, Council of Light that are supporting you at all times in the fulfillment of your best possible life. They are always helping us and acting on our best behalf.

I'm excited for you to get to know them for yourself. The more you understand how to access your higher states of consciousness, the more you will sense the wonderful world of your Tribe of Light and all the ways they can help you. Your personal Tribe of Light is one of your greatest life resources.

Now let's begin by learning how to shift your state of consciousness and activate your intuition to meet your personal Tribe of Light.

THE LIGHT BODY

Your light body lives within your etheric body, which enfolds your physical body. It's often seen as a white etheric orb of light around the physical body, and can measure a person's vitality of spiritual life force. Your light body communicates through your nervous system, which is based on electricity. This is not the same as the aura which is represented in colors that communicate the emotional reactions of a person and their environment.

The light body can travel in a vehicle of consciousness known as the merkabah or star tetrahedron. This is a vehicle of light based on sacred geometry, which is a formula of energy universal creation abides by. The light body is an exact replica of you in physical form, also known as your etheric double or twin.

It's the part of your consciousness that can astral travel through time, space, and dimensions. It is the electronic light body substance created from electrons, the building blocks of the Universe. Your light body never dies or ages. It holds your cellular memories from life time to life time and also retains the consciousness of your Soul Blueprint and spirit wisdom.

It is the part of your consciousness that is the communicator between the dimensional bodies. To enhance your light body, one technique that can assist you greatly is noticing how far away the etheric white orb of energy is from your physical body. This is easiest to sense with your eyes closed. Then through the power of your breath, you energetically push or pull this orb of light gently around you until it is within two to four feet of you.

If the orb is expanded beyond that length, it's counter intuitive but empaths actually do better and will feel safer in the world when they expand their energy as far as possible. Try going out fifteen feet first, then go for fifty feet, next try sending your energy out around the Earth. It's easier to clear energy the more expanded your energy field is and you can sense more around you more accurately. You'll also feel like you can breathe again and have a little elbow room to experience your own feelings and thoughts more clearly.

It's interesting to begin sending your light body to another location and watch the world from its perception. Some of my favorite ways to practice this include imagining I'm in the eyes of a bird flying high above me viewing the landscape below, or entering into a sacred place and sensing all that has gone on before me, or traveling to the future to see a projected vision of an outcome I'm curious about.

Healers that use the light body as their instrument of healing will usually scan the physical body for pranic strength and energetic blockages. They often prefer accessing electrical impulses above the body to correct imbalances instead of using direct touch.

A person's light body is an amazing consciousness that can travel, expand, contract, heal, sense, integrate, and balance. Through this energetic field that's around you and everything in existence (even inanimate objects), you can realize that you are, in some way, touching all of life.

Your electrical body is the light energy that acts as a battery of electrical currents in your heart, brain, nervous system, and meridian system. It's important to keep your nervous system strong and healthy when doing energy work, healing work, clairvoyant work, personal growth, soul travel, and release work. Really, it's important to keep it strong when dealing with life in general.

Raising children, sitting in traffic, even dealing with environmental toxicity, relationships, job stress, change, moves, and other daily challenges require nurturing and maintaining a strong nervous system. Otherwise you may find yourself shutting down, shrinking your energy field, feeling anxiety, getting overwhelmed and over-reacting to people.

Consulting with a nutritionist or reading nutritional books is a great place to learn what the nervous system needs to be healthy, wealthy, and wise. And remember to always drink lots of water because water is a conductor of electricity.

Your ability to handle your life is as strong as your nervous system. All the information in your entire reality— including the worlds you access above or around you— must travel through the super highway of your nervous system. It is the great storyteller of all your unconscious thoughts and feelings.

Your nervous system not only receives electrical currents from your environment and the collective unconscious of overlapping energy fields, but continually vibrates information from your subconscious outward into your reality as well. Your subconscious is like a library holding all your stories while your nervous system tells the stories.

How those stories get stored in the library of your subconscious happens when you have experiences that you don't have the consciousness to deal with such as a trauma, judgment, fear or projection from a person you have given your personal power to. Likewise, when you have a conscious realization or return to love, acceptance, forgiveness or gratitude, it can clear any unresolved issues so that you are living your dharma (life purpose) instead of karma (action/reaction).

Your Healing Journey

I've seen a lot of people engage in a healing journey (either as healer or to be healed) and get burned out. Be aware that any healing process and self-growth work—even fulfilling your destiny—requires an enormous amount of energy on every level of your being. People get halfway through, wondering if there will ever be an end to it all. They just want to give up on their journeys.

We just didn't realize that every cell in our bodies would start to cleanse, that all the toxicity could cause a bloating, and that the sheath around our nervous systems would become even thinner. We can become so sensitive that even going shopping becomes a big deal. To top it off, our financial situation can reflect this inner turmoil; with every issue we trigger, we play it out in our money.

Support of the Nervous System

Taking care of your nervous system and light body will allow you to more easily and gracefully become cosmic units in a world community. Start by supporting your physical body and nervous system. When you call in spiritual energy from within you, around you, or above you, you will begin bringing in an immense amount of light, remember to ground this energy into the core of the planet. Your energy is like a battery, batteries need to be grounded to work properly.

This light— whether it comes from within your cells, from a healer or healing process, or from an Angel or Being of Light—will pass electrically through your nervous system. It allows your light body to integrate lost vital life force into its innate state while passing through your nervous system in the form of electricity. Because this electricity acts as battery cables that carry a charge, you must be strong enough to handle large volts of energy. Otherwise, it could cause you to short circuit and burn out on your quest for the life you were meant to lead.

Remember that the nervous system is the communication center for more than the light body. It's the center for the glandular system, the chakras, and the organs they affect. When you get burned out, past or chronic weaknesses tend to get triggered first. These could include emotional traumas, stuck thought forms, cellular memories from past lives, physical injuries, and more. I suggest you keep strengthening your nervous system by drinking plenty of clean water, standing barefoot on the Earth as often as possible and getting lots of rest.

Let It All Go

It takes an enormous amount of energy to heal, which is why more people don't embrace healing. They have just enough day-to-day energy to sustain the illusions they created (and/or were projected onto as a child) to survive.

Having enough energy to heal is only half of the problem. The other half is the willingness to let it all go. Most people don't take kindly to the thought of surrender. It tends to trigger a fight-or-flight syndrome.

Let me ask you these questions about your healing journey:

- What would it take to be and live as my highest vibrational resonance?

- What would it take for me to lay down my burdens and turn it over to the Divine Mind, the Heart of All Creation, Source Energy, the Universe and my Tribe of Light in service to my soul's journey?

- What would it take for my life to be easy, joyful, graceful and abundant?

Gratitude is a big one to add to this.

I'm grateful for my life, I'm grateful for .... Fill in the blanks as many times a day as possible.

It's amazing how we think we want something *until we can really have it*. Our emotions and thought forms are addictive behavior patterns that become so familiar to us, we're afraid to let them go—perhaps because we don't know how to do things differently. We have forgotten to access the resources that can help us. This is where your dimensional selves and Tribes of Light Beings come into play.

Returning to Your Divine Source

If you're willing, I suggest using a simple clearing technique that can help you move through any blocks in your nervous system easily and gracefully. It will prevent you from burning out as you rediscover your soul's magnificence.

Universal Law: *Your consciousness creates your reality.*

Consciousness is the part of mind that allows you to perceive what's around you. The more expanded your consciousness, the more compassionate and wise your perception. If your consciousness is jumbled up with other people's projections and emotions, you become lost in a sea of discordant chaos and overwhelm. You have no clue about who you are or what your original intention was in having this human experience. You've lost touch with your authentic self who carries the wisdom of your love, your inner authority to make things happen, and your soul's magnificence to express the gifts you came to give. The simplest way to return back to your own inner soul rhythm and clear your head, heart, body, or spirit is to focus on breathing through your heart center. Notice the rhythm of your breathing rising and falling. Notice your heart beat. Then notice the heartbeat of the Universe. You will soon start to come into a one heart breath which brings you into coherence with your head and heart as well as Universal

Flow. This normally only takes three to twelve breaths to re-center yourself. It will feel like you just clicked back into place.

It's easy to get out of rhythm with yourself by focusing our awareness on outside stimuli or events. When we don't re-align our consciousness back to our inner rhythm, we get out of our perfect zone. Breath is the prana of Source Energy, it is a healing instrument. It's filled with the electronic substance of Source Energy, Pure Love and Light, which sustains supplies, protects, and illumines us within our life journey.

Breathing is free and easy. Naturally, it should be done everywhere you go. Breathing enlivens the body, calms the soul, inspires the mind, and frees the spirit; it is simply one of the greatest resources you have to heal anything that ails you.

"You are Here"

To assess "where you are" on this map of consciousness, start by finding the locator that says "you are here" with a big yellow arrow, just like a directional map in an amusement park. To do that, simply focus on your breathing for a moment and then notice your emotional state; it will take you immediately to the yellow "you are here" arrow.

Noticing your emotional reaction to the world around you lets you know the reflection of your subconscious and the breathing will bring you back home to your own inner rhythm. You can then reference your location on the map of consciousness and get back on path with the journey of your Soul Blueprint.

Once you have re-centered, you are much better equipped to know what you need in the present moment in the form of life tools, power sources, and spiritual assistants that can help you on your path. They can be blue flaming swords, shields of light, gate keepers in the form of totem animals, Angels that bring you healing elixirs, even worm holes to enter into other dimensions. Doesn't this sound like fun? Those souls who like the latest greatest gadget may especially enjoy exploring this consciousness journey because of all the cool tools and Beings of Light you get to play with along the way.

Communication Super Highway

The nervous system is like a satellite dish that can pick up an infinite number of "stations," making it the super highway for all communication that passes through you. Your nervous system has an encoding process, much like the one shown in the movie "The Matrix" with Keanu Reeves. When you learn to read this encoding by being present to your Light Body, you can navigate through your illusions effortlessly. That's when the world starts to make a whole lot more sense.

That's because the Light Body knows how to interpret the emotions and thoughts that energetically affect you in everything you do. Your nervous system picks up most of its "stations" through the aura. The aura in turn governs your emotional responses to people and the environment, like the human version of cat whiskers. It senses other energetic fields in people's emotions and thought forms, including the feeling in a house, being in nature, and other energetic phenomena such as electrical energy fields radiating from computers, sound waves, ghosts, and more. When this sensory input is picked up by your aura, it's also picked up by your Light Body, and the information enters your nervous system.

This describes a form of intuition called "empathing." Empathing means if it's an emotion or thought form from another person or group, then your emotional body may "empath" that information as if you yourself were thinking or feeling it.

It can be scary to see how connected people really are to each other. When I figured this out, I didn't bother lying anymore; I realized others already knew the truth even if they weren't 100 percent conscious of it. Similarly, if a person is depressed, you may sense it, even though he or she hasn't told you.

If you're not able to distinguish between your own feelings and theirs, you might feel depressed the rest of the day. This is also true with thought forms. If others are thinking they are stupid or unlovable, you may start thinking that way about yourself or them when that's not how you really feel at all. Thoughts and emotions come together as a package deal. When you have a feeling, a thought form will follow to validate it with a belief system, and a thought will generate a feeling to validate it with an emotional response.

The Process of "Empathing"

As noted earlier, how you perceive and create the world around you comes through the great story teller, your nervous system, which helped you survive as a child. You'd listen to other people's stories by "empathing" their thoughts and emotions to know how to respond for love, attention, help, food, and so on.

This process actually started in your mother's womb and "downloaded" into your unconscious as an unborn infant. Right from conception, your nervous system has been adopting your mother's and father's thought forms, emotions, and environmental activity in addition to genetic encoding from your lineage.

Empathing is communicating through emotional transference and telepathy, which is an animal's main form of communication. Because this gift begins in childhood, you can easily access it through your inner child. Doing inner child healing often requires consciously going back into your childhood to determine where you got stuck in an emotional expression or thought pattern.

It correlates to an early experience you didn't understand. As a child, you assessed the situation and developed a protective behavior pattern to cope with an event that is usually fear based. But your childhood assessments and protective behavior patterns may no longer serve you as an adult. As a matter of fact, they usually work *against* your ability to connect with others in a loving, trusting way. They can stop you from living the life you were meant to live.

You've probably noticed the innocence of small children. They say exactly the truth of what's going on without a second thought. If you could see people's auras, you'd know exactly how they're feeling.

Or if you were telepathic, you could instantly read their minds. That's what children do—only they don't know they're doing it. Most children have not matured this gift to its next evolution of intuition within the soul.

Consequently, they don't know how to discern the difference between the projected feelings of another and their own true feelings in the moment. The projections and feelings of others can overwhelm them if they don't realize what's happening.

Projection of Others

As a child, if you weren't taught emotional acceptance—if you weren't told that you are always safe and unconditionally loved for whom you truly are—then it's easy to get caught up in the projections of others. You'd then develop different forms of protection to distance yourself from all the projections constantly conveyed by parents and other people.

What are projections? They are unresolved emotional conflicts backed up by stories they create about what's real in a person's world. Projections rarely have anything to do with reality. They are defense mechanisms that the human mind creates to protect itself from painful experiences.

Even though you're not a child, these projections constantly bombard you from the people around you. Guess what? You're constantly bombarding *them* with your projections, too. In reality, you're still highly telepathic and can instantly read a person's emotional state.

Everyone has this gift—not just a few you believe are psychically gifted— but everyone. This gift is fully intact; you probably just don't realize you're using it all the time. It's like being a fish in water; the fish doesn't know it's in the water until it's taken out of it.

How does it all work? Your subconscious mind sends a story of unresolved pain and suffering to your nervous system every day, causing you to keep recreating your past until it's resolved. You have repeating experiences, just like Bill Murray's character did in the movie *Groundhog Day*.

Remember, your subconscious mind helps you heal—that's its job. It continually tells your nervous system to put you in similar situations and with people who reflect your past. That pattern won't change until you have called back your power and are once again in divine alignment within yourself.

Experiences of Your Inner Child

I suggest making friends with your innocent, truth-telling inner child. When you do, you'll realize how intuitive you really are. When you first listen to your inner child, you let your emotions come to the surface in a way that allows you to feel in control. People don't usually *want* to befriend their inner child because it remembers all the unresolved problems and fears of their childhood. Sometimes it reminds them how inadequate and wrong they felt, like the character Bruce Willis played in the movie *The Kid*.

When you get stuck in negative emotional states, it drains your life force and lowers your immune system. Listening to your inner child is an excellent technique for giving your emotional body a place to be heard. It also provides a resource for resolving conflict within you, and assists you back to a state of peace easily and effortlessly. As a result, your nervous system can create a new result instead of continuing to recreate the unresolved conflict you may be feeling.

A Simple Clearing Technique

First, begin by breathing into your heart center. Notice how you feel in the moment and allow yourself to identify any feeling that's pulsing through your light body. Next, continue to keep breathing into this emotion and let your light body guide you to where it's being stored in the physical body.

Ask your light body to assist you in releasing this emotion into your heart center. Once you feel like you're present to the depth of this emotion within your heart center, you transmute this emotional energy into a conscious feeling that your soul's wisdom can now assist you in releasing. Ask your soul's wisdom and an angel to guide you to the source of this feeling.

At first, you'll notice the most recent place this feeling was triggered in you. Simply breathe all the way into that feeling and allow yourself to become *one* with the feeling, making it more fully integrated. Then ask your inner child to guide you back to the very first memory you have where this feeling was present. Notice the precise memory being brought to your awareness. Don't question or judge it; just sit with it and ask your soul's wisdom and an angel to show you the truth of this memory.

Once you've seen its truth, you're ready to let it go. You're ready to gain your soul's wisdom about this experience and move on, so you don't have to keep replaying out this memory over and over with people in your life today. Ask your soul's wisdom and an angel to bring you a resource to assist you in healing this experience. Place this gift of knowing in a safe place.

The light body then takes this healed energy and brings it back into your electrical body to increase your consciousness, strength and well-being. The dimensional bodies are inseparable and their activities will overlap with one another.

THE SOUL'S JOURNEY

The soul, who holds the perfected feeling of our life experiences, governs the sacred heart. Your soul is the energetic part of you that's living the journey. When you are present to your soul, colors are brighter; life is more beautiful, sensual, and vivid. You live in the present moment. You take time to smell the roses.

Communication to the soul flows easiest through your heart center, known as your heart's wisdom. In your heart's wisdom, you can understand deeper feelings about your life experiences so you can integrate them as a healing and blessing, bringing you into a state of wholeness. By integrating your life experiences into wholeness, your soul assists you with being in integrity with the whole Universe; you can achieve alignment spiritually, mentally, emotionally, and physically.

Emotional State

Most of the time, people identify their life experiences from an emotional state. This approach is reactionary to life instead of experiential. When you experience something in the present moment through the soul, you feel peaceful, compassionate, and understanding. You know an infinite intelligence governs things, which allows you the space of graceful surrender to the highest good.

Emotions change constantly like water. They are expressed in your aura through the nervous system by the inner-child self. Like a cat's whiskers, they tell you "what's up" in your environment. In contrast, your feelings indicate how you're actually being affected by an experience in the moment.

Weave the Stories

Many events can happen to a person from the time they incarnate on this Earth until they leave it. But one thing is for certain—you will touch others' lives profoundly as theirs will touch yours. People weave stories of wisdom into each other's living tapestries. And at some point, you realize that by unconditionally giving your gift to the world, the most profound gift has been the journey itself. You'll also realize that the lives you so deeply touched—and those that have deeply touched you—have shifted the fabric of your world.

Your soul helps you integrate your life experiences so you can evolve from the story-telling or wisdom of each one.

You thread the wisdom you gain into your tapestry; the more threads of wisdom you have, the more easily can you see your Soul

Blueprint. No matter how different each person's journey is—woven with different-colored threads into unique tapestries—the eternal truth hidden within them is much the same for all of us.

What do all of us see when the tapestry is complete? A being of Divine Love who knows the eternal truth of existence which is simply *to love and be love*. Love is the essence of the gift you give on behalf of Spirit.

A Gift of Love

When you came down through the dimensions of consciousness to give this gift of love, you came into human form and ignited the journey of your Soul Blueprint. Every day, as the spark of love ignites, the magnificence of your soul burns brightly, igniting within others the remembrance of their unique gifts of love.

We all come from one, we all come from love, we are love in this moment, and we shall all return to love. That's the soul's journey, and the fulfillment of our destiny is when we have the courage to show up and unconditionally express the gift that lives within our soul's magnificence. Destiny is when you have reached the destination of peace inside yourself, which can be at any given moment.

As long as we can remember this eternal truth hidden within our tapestry, the journey will always be compassionately graceful. When we begin to drift into a forgetful slumber, letting the eternal truth that we are "love in form" begin to slip away from us—our lives reflect it with stress, depression, anger, fear, unhappiness, loneliness, chaos, poor health, and money issues. The list goes on and on. Then our souls will create opportunities to awaken, and get back on track with our original intentions.

Sometimes it will take years for our souls to unravel the parable of the story, depending on how deeply we hide the fear or pain. But our soul will never leave our side. They will bring in assistance through our Higher Self and our Tribe of Light to help when we're ready to remember the eternal truth again.

How My Own Journey Began

I was fifteen years old and living in Atlanta, Georgia, with my mother and stepfather. My father had died in a bicycle accident nine months earlier. The loss of him in my life had gone much deeper than I was willing to admit. Subconsciously, I think I was setting things up to check out, but my soul wouldn't tolerate that.

It was during this time after his death that I had become more reckless with my behavior than I'd ever been. One cold drizzly day in January, I had skipped school. For most of the morning I slept in my car parked outside of the house of friends who were older than me. Late in the morning, one of the guys in the house woke me up.

We drove to the high school to pick up Jill, a friend I had been waiting to meet up with since the beginning of my day. We saw her walking down the road after school got out. I pulled over and she jumped into the back seat. I had something to pick up at the grocery store for my mother, so they said they'd go with me.

As I was driving around a curve on Monroe Road near Peachtree Street in midtown Atlanta, another car came toward me too far over into my lane. Adjusting for it, I swerved. My car began to hydroplane on the road still wet from the recent rain. At that moment, everything began moving in slow motion—as if all time and space stood still. Everything was silent in my head except the Bob Dylan song playing in the background. Then all of a sudden, BAM! We hit a telephone pole. It was on my side of the car, right behind my seat.

My world completely went black for about thirty seconds. As soon as I came back into focus, I asked if everyone was all right. My friend in the front seat said he thought he was okay, but his back hurt. No reply came from the back seat. I realized the whole driver's side door had been smashed in. I squeezed through the broken window and tried to get to Jill who was out cold in the back seat.

I tried to pull her out of the passenger side, but she was stuck. I ran to a house across the street to get help. My friend stayed behind with Jill. When I got back, she opened her eyes briefly and looked at me. She didn't say a word. I told her we'd get her out in minute. "Just hang on," I pleaded. "It will be okay." I saw her pupils dilate and she drifted out of consciousness again.

The street cleaner was the first person to arrive on the scene to clean up the glass. I thought, "How weird. This isn't a good sign." The ambulance and police showed up next. The EMS people rescued Jill from the car and had her lying on the street. I quickly slipped into a frantic state of scattered feelings. I desperately felt that I had to do something to help save her or I would lose control of myself completely.

A policeman was trying to get information from me, but all I wanted to do was stay beside Jill. I just knew if I could place my hands on her, or kiss her like Snow White in the childhood fairy tale, she would wake up and everything would be all right again. It was such a powerful, immortal feeling that anything was possible. And yet, at the same time, I felt so utterly powerless to do anything at all.

Before I had the courage to reach over and touch her, the EMS people rushed her off in the ambulance. The police led me over to the patrol car with them, and had me sit inside it. Because Jill was a minor, they needed her mother's consent for whatever they thought they'd have to do for her. I figured they must have found Jill's mom quickly because the search ended after about fifteen minutes. But that wasn't why. Jill had died in the ambulance.

They had to take me to the police station and charge me with vehicular homicide. I remember my mother walking in the front door of the police station. I didn't know what to say to her. I could hardly believe what I'd done until they took me into another room.

There stood Jill's mother, a woman I'd never met. She held her head in her hands as she cried silently. She looked up when I came in and just said, "At least Jill didn't die alone mugged on the street. She was with someone who loved her." I tried to say I was sorry, but how could I ever say "sorry" deeply enough? I was responsible for taking away this woman's only child. I became speechless, immersed in a shock of horror.

I know now that it was in the midst of this tragic accident that I lost faith in myself and in God. I didn't have the resources to choose to love deeply in the face of such fear and trauma. I didn't know how to put all my faith in the miracle of life. Instead I found myself desperately struggling to come to terms with losing someone whom I cared deeply about to the hand of death, all the while knowing that what was most unbearable was the realization that as the driver it was *at my hand* that she got hurt.

Sleeping, Dreaming

The charges for vehicular homicide were dropped in court, but the feeling remained of having been responsible for the death of someone I loved dearly. They let me leave the police station with my mother. All I wanted to do was sleep, which is exactly what I did for the next six months.

The night of the accident, I had a lucid dream I'll never forget. I was in the woods by a lake; all was quiet and peaceful. I saw Jill coming through the woods toward me. She never spoke a word; she just looked serene as she gently smiled at me. I began to cry as I was telling her I was so sorry for what had happened, that I had never meant to hurt her. We walked up to an open log tavern.

When I knew our time was almost over, I asked if I could kiss her goodbye. She nodded yes. I think I still believed that a "Snow White" kiss would somehow break the spell and bring her back. I held her close and hugged her goodbye after which she turned and walked into a bright, glowing column of light. I knew she would be okay and that, in her eyes, there wasn't anything to be forgiven for.

But inside my own heart, none of this mattered. When I woke up, all I wanted to do was go back to sleep. Perhaps I could find Jill again, and find a way to make it all right. I paid a heavy price because I slept through all of eleventh grade, failing everything. My mother tried taking me to a counselor, but it was useless. I quit school when I was sixteen and moved out on my own, getting odd jobs here and there to get by.

Soul Searching

During that time, I couldn't stand the thought of feeling stupid from quitting school, plus, I didn't trust a word anyone in authority had to say. So one day, it came to me to learn to communicate with the soul. Everyone has a soul. It can't be destroyed, it never lies, and it always knows what to do in any situation. I focused all my attention on learning how to communicate with my soul.

I started studying chakras, astral projection, astrology, lucid dreaming, crystals, communication with fairies and tree spirits, core energetics, psychic abilities, and so on. All of it was interesting, but none of it provided the connection to my soul I so desperately sought.

Finally, one day when I was twenty-one and had a job in a health food store, I saw a flyer about Reiki Healing on the bulletin board. I called the number listed and went that week for my first initiation with a Reiki master. That was it. Everything clicked into place for me.

My intuition opened up. I'd lay my hands on a person and they would instantly heat up and I would experience visions. I knew I had full communication with people's souls. All I wanted to do was lay my hands on people. I took a Jin Shin Jitsu class on oriental healing, figuring I must be a hands-on healer. Then I enrolled in massage school shortly after that. I began seeing clearly into people's bodies and started practicing to be a healer.

While attending massage school, I decided to get certified for the second level of Reiki. This time, I found a woman who became my spiritual mentor for the next seven years. She gave me the confidence to fully expand my vision. I finished Reiki Level Three, did Native American sweat lodges, became initiated into the realm of psychic surgeons known as spirit doctors, and began studying the Flower of Life by Drunvalo Mechezidech.

Before long, I began having full blown kundalini experiences. Then my Reiki teacher introduced me to all the "worlds within worlds" in which we live—and showed me how to communicate with the beings that lived in these worlds. This is when I learned to communicate with the Angels—and they've been my best friends ever since.

In the Presence of Angels

When I was in the presence of the Angels, I felt a deep peace and sense of safety I'd never known before. My intuitive skills kept expanding, and through the Angels, I began seeing emotions, childhood stories, past lives, and other people's Angels and guides. The Angels could even tell me how the person I was working on could heal issues or directly communicate with their Angels.

As my skill level grew, I felt ready for the next step and interviewed for a position at an alternative health center. That's where I met my second spiritual mentor. My two teachers couldn't have been more different in their approach to healing. I went from studying Angels, past lives, and Ascended Masters to diving headfirst into the emotional body of the inner child, unconscious thought forms, and projections of parents and genetic lineage. There, I learned that "consciousness creates reality." I learned to begin healing and shifting results in the present moment by listening deeply to unresolved emotions and thought forms of a person's inner child.

Strangely, when I first got the job at the center, all I could do again was sleep—all the time. I suppose I was finally starting to clean up the mess from my past.

My Journey into Healing

Over the next four and a half years, I did hands-on Reiki initiations and intuitive sessions, and taught classes. I did body readings, flower essence readings, and aura readings. Eventually, I was interviewed on CNN Headline News, several radio talk programs, and on local public access television in regards to my intuitive abilities. I had finally found a way to express my gifts to a broad spectrum of people.

"It's All About the Love."

Toward the end of three years at the healing center, I went on a teaching tour in Russia, giving Reiki initiations and soul readings in Saint Petersburg, Moscow, and Novosibirsk, Siberia. I must have given more than one hundred Reiki initiations in three weeks—an awesome, life-changing experience.

My Gratitude

As part of my journey, I offer this book of soul teachings in gratitude and adoration to all who have weaved a thread of wisdom into the tapestry of my life. I'm grateful to all the Angels and Beings of Light who have guided me, to my mother for her gift of intuition and unconditional love, to my father for being a master teacher of spiritual power and compassion, to Jill who initiated me into the path of my Soul Blueprint. And to all of you who are my soul family on this Dharma Path with me, so that we may all open to the remembrance of the eternal truth hidden within our own unique tapestry of light.

Your Soul Gifts

You have soul gifts and quality essences that represent the basic core of who you are beyond your personality. When you know your soul gifts and the quality essence of who you truly are, they become tools in the fulfillment of your soul's journey. If you don't identify these gifts and essences, they often work *against* you instead of *for* you. It's like having a powerful sword in your service, but if you don't know how to wield it, you quickly realize it has two sides.

Soul gifts include your ability to heal the human heart, be patient with others, hold a space of unconditional love, and listen deeply. Soul gifts can be the gift of humor, insight, empathy, truth, loyalty, joy, wisdom, spiritual "warriorism", etc. Soul gifts are your gift of love through unconditional service to others. Quality essences are traits that others can feel coming from you—peace, compassion, nurturance, strength—so that when others are in your presence, they sit in the radiance of your lightness of being. You don't have to go to school to learn it; it lives innately within you and you develop your soul gifts in the journey of life.

When you're not in touch with your quality essences, you may feel like you're sitting in the shadow of your truth. Quality essences resonate from your beingness, acting as a blessing to all of life. Your soul gifts are divine activities of service.

It's actually easy to become aware of your soul gifts and quality essences through simple observation of yourself. If you give yourself the space to see your truth through the eyes of your soul, it's more than obvious. Others around you can often identify this in you easily. "Who you are" is really no secret; it's just a matter of being willing to own your soul's magnificence. Ask your soul to show you the truth of your soul gifts and quality essence. You may find that you already know the answer; you probably haven't had it reflected back to you in a loving way that you could understand it.

Retreating from Life

When we don't know how to handle situations (especially when we are children), then we tend to rise above our body energetically and retreat from life. When this happens, it's hard for us to tell people how we feel or what we want. It's like we're not "home" any more.

We then begin handling life on automatic pilot. Sure, we get up and function in ways that are expected of us. But we're no longer present to situations in the current moment. Instead, we become disassociated from ourselves and others. We have fragments of our self that we selectively bring forward and other parts that we keep hidden from the world, depending on our level of safety or fear.

Several types of work address this disassociate behaviorism, including inner child work, hypnosis, soul retrieval work, and transpersonal psychology, just to name a few. I'm sure many forms of therapy can help. However, using the power of your breath to reconnect you into your body can do wonders. It's a matter of staying present in difficult situations and not checking out.

Resolving Issues

Ask your soul's wisdom to assist you in resolving issues. Indeed, your soul can help you with everything. It can tap into the higher sources of information and ground them for you. It always knows the best solutions because it has based its truth in your heart—and humans are all beings of the heart. Your soul is gifted with finding ways of win/win solutions and conflict resolutions that are simple and true to the heart. You can't lose once you have learned to listen to and trust your soul.

Keep in mind your soul is the part of your having a "feeling" experience on planet Earth. It loves communion, whether it's in community with others, nature, God, the Angels, or more. It loves to be in the present moment and connect deeply with whatever lies in its space.

The soul—by its very nature—tends to be healing, creative, sensual, peaceful, and unconditionally loving. It houses itself within your heart center in its communication with you and others. If you want to access your soul's wisdom in a particular situation or meditation, focus your awareness on your heart center. Your soul knows the truth of what anyone is feeling at any given time; it knows the best way to be present.

More than that, the soul doesn't react; it *is* present and in the moment. Breathing rhythmically through your heart center and expanding it outward can entrain your heart into a state of compassion. It helps to focus on a happy thought or memory and engage your heart to open fully.

This expansion of your heart in a state of love, adoration, and gratitude will increase your immune system, your sense of abundance, your higher consciousness, and your intuition—among many other gifts. When you send out a positive vibration of this entrainment of compassion, you're influencing all of life around you to respond to you in love, regardless of the situation. Use it as a powerful tool of co-creation through unconditional love.

Awakening the Soul Meditation

To connect to the presence of your soul, take several deep breaths in and out of your heart center focusing your awareness on connecting to your heart's wisdom. Once you feel this connection, begin to expand into the radiance of light that is shining forth from your heart center, this is the jewel of your soul's love.

Ask your soul to guide you into this Temple of Light, known as the Sacred Heart. As you enter into the Temple of your Sacred Heart, notice the magnificence of your soul's beauty and light, the sacred sounds of peace that resonate from it's unique soul note, and its mystical quality essences and strengths. Let your soul guide you into a Sacred Heart Healing Chamber of Light for rejuvenation and healing.

Relax into this chamber of light, ask your soul to guide you through the journey of your destiny, from the time you were conceived, until this present moment, revealing to you the wisdom of your life journey that will allow you to release certain events you had not understood before, or the higher purpose of certain people in your life, on a movie screen before you. You may want to ask your soul questions that will assist you in your daily life - like how to live in the present moment, what are your soul gifts, and how can you live a life of peace. Your soul's wisdom can assist you in any life issue you may experience to have a loving outcome.

THE HIGHER SELF

The Higher Self—who holds the perfected vision of our life experiences—governs our Higher Mental Body above our head. Often seen as a brilliant white light, it acts as the access point into higher wisdom, truth, understanding, and compassion. Like the enlightened guru sitting on the mountaintop looking out over our life journeys, the Higher Self guides us in ways our human self and personality aren't able to see from their limited perspective.

The Higher Self is also known as the Sacred Archetype. Our Sacred Archetype is like the digital image of the Higher Self. You can create a sacred healing chamber in your inner mind. This is usually a place in nature or another dimension that feels sacred and peaceful for you to give and receive healing energy to yourself or others.

Once you feel comfortable in your sacred healing chamber, Invite in your Sacred Archetype. The Sacred Archetype is the part of your Higher Self that carries all your souls wisdom gained from other lifetimes, dimensions, worlds. It also has sacred and magical objects that have been meaningful throughout other experiences such as crystals, gemstones, crystal balls, the clothes it wears, jewelry, crowns, head garments, staffs, swords, totem animals, books, libraries, etc.

Once you have looked closely at your Sacred Archetype, begin to how it feels to you, the soul attributes, such as wisdom, peace, love, strength, power, compassion, clarity, etc.

Then come into a tender embrace, like a hug, and breathe in and out three to ten times until you feel at one and integrated with your Sacred Archetype. Once you feel one with your Sacred Archetype, move through the world as your Sacred Archetype and notice how your feel. Do you feel more empowered, at peace, wiser, and more loving. This will affect your self-confidence, self-love, self-worth, and the world will respond positively with you.

Behavior Patterns

The human mind represents your personality. Behavior patterns that give you "personality" are usually created from what your mind has seen before. This causes you to behave in mannerisms—as you felt, heard, or saw your mother, father, or another significant authority figure behave. As a child, you were likely taught subconsciously to give over your inner authority to the people who raised you. As an infant, you perceived that your survival depended on them instead of the Divine Presence within you. This conditioning of human nature is rampant in religion, politics, business, and life in general.

By re-connecting to your Higher Self, you're returning to your ability to see only the highest truth in any situation. It gets you back to your original guidance system of your Higher Self— the innate system designed to guide you in the life you were meant to live. It steers you through the perfected vision versus the life you were told you should (or shouldn't) live.

Guidance from Your Higher Self

When you give your power to another human being such as a parent or loved one, you set yourself up to live by another person's strengths, weaknesses, and fear-based limitations. You begin to lose touch with your own strengths and weaknesses that your soul is here to experience.

Your mission is to fulfill the journey of your own unique Divine Blueprint. That means when you lose yourself in another person's projections of life, you limit your potential by half of what you're capable of. But when you live by the guidance of your Higher Self, you live in the full potential of the perfected vision you were meant to live. This is Divine Grace in action!

Why constantly feel inadequate trying to live within someone else's projection? You don't have the resources or information to deal with the person's soul journey; it simply isn't yours to do. Your internal guidance system through your Higher Self is only meant to guide your personal journey.

Within that journey, you automatically assist others with your Higher Self's wisdom and compassion. When you live in another's projection, then you feel responsible and overwhelmed for things you have no governing power over. To help you change this perception, begin shifting from the "human" mind to the "higher" mind.

You can do this by saying "I am allowing the rays of my higher self to guide me today."

The "Human" Mind

The brain, which is governed by personality, is the electrical motor of the mind and perceives conscious reality in this world. The Higher Mental Body, which is governed by your Higher Self, perceives your expanded consciousness and is seen as a crown of light around your head also referred to as a halo that others can actually see when the consciousness of enlightenment is high enough. Your Higher Mental Body perceives reality from a universal understanding and perfected visions; it isn't limited to the physical body. The human mind constantly responds to the perception of the environment and how to survive.

Based on what the human mind perceives, it sends out hormones and chemicals into the blood stream to produce validating results such as stress, overwhelm, fear, worry, guilt. So if you meditate and connect to your Higher Self, your brain will perceive this reality and sends out hormones that produce the results of balance, peacefulness, harmony and people who are compatible with you.

If, as a child, you looked to your parents to show you how to survive in the world, then your brain perceives through the personality and subconscious issues. Consequently, it will always have limited viewpoints, because it's based on unresolved fear patterns you learned as a child. From this limited view point of fear, pain, and suffering, your brain locks into this reality and keeps sending signals that produce the hormones that create specific results to validate this perception.

The human mind—a creature of habit that mostly dwells in the past—isn't nearly as creative as people give it credit for. The higher mind, though, is capable of infinite possibilities. That's why Einstein, Mozart, and Da Vinci all had ways of expanding beyond the human mind of limitations and expanding into the higher mind of unlimited resources.

Focus on Breathing

The human mind was designed to serve the higher mind's direction. If you've put the human mind in charge of your life, you're letting unresolved conflicts and fear-based projections run your life. By focusing your awareness on breathing in and out of your heart center, you can disengage from your human mind's activity and connect with the heart's wisdom of the soul—which connects to the higher wisdom of the Higher Self.

They coordinate with one another so that a shift from the human mind into the higher mind flows gracefully through the channel of the heart. Tapping into the power of breath is an ancient art of divine alchemy practiced by the masters to shift states of consciousness, increase pranic life force, heal the body, and govern the secretion of hormones into your blood stream. You can use it to help you govern your responses to life.

Your Higher Self is the part of you that is the Sacred Archetype & the Divine Alchemist, who possess all the wisdom gained from all your life experiences, including past lives and other dimensional lives.

When you stay connected with your Higher Self, you will walk this Earth as a living master. You will develop the ability to see life through the eyes of compassion, access the Divine Mind of Creation. Your Higher Self can show pictures or speak about the perfected vision of your life path or specific experiences you want guidance on. Use it as your own private counsel or life coach.

Be sure to begin your day by breathing through your heart. Once you feel centered in your heart center, focus your awareness on connecting to your Higher Self, a brilliant white light of inner authority above your head. When you feel this connection, ask your Higher Self to show you the perfected plan for the day or for an event. It will show you the perfected vision to support your life path with grace and gratitude.

The Higher Self is extremely fair in all circumstances. Even if you don't understand at the time what you're being shown, just trust it. Remember, your Higher Self not only knows your past, present, and future, but also those of others. It teaches you how to respond with the highest compassion and wisdom with others.

Receiving this information may feel a little awkward because it's different than the habit of your personality's response. Like any new habit, it takes getting used to. But when you start seeing the results of synchronistic miracles and harmonious perfection playing out, you will be happy you created this relationship with your Higher Self.

Igniting the Crown of Light Meditation

Breathing gently into your heart area, allow your sacred heart to expand. When you feel connected to your heart rhythm, focus your awareness on the top of your head. Call forth to your Higher Self to enfold you in the Higher Mental Body. Begin to notice the lightness of being and clarity of mind that comes from being connected here. Ask your Higher Self to show you the crown of light that enfolds your head.

The crown of light is a seven-pointed crown each reflecting the colors of the universal rays which are from your right to left: pink, sunshine yellow, blue, crystal white, green, violet, and ruby. The rays of light represent the universal rays of co-creation governed by the Mighty Elohim Angels.

Ask your Higher Self to show you your Sacred Healing Chamber. This will usually be a peaceful place in nature or another dimension. Observe your surroundings, find a comfortable place.

Ask your Higher Self to reveal itself to you as the image of the Sacred Archetype. Notice all the unique things about your Sacred Archetype such as the clothing style, color of skin and eyes, is it wearing any crystals, gemstones, jewelry, head ornament, staff, sword, shields, books, scrolls, totem animals, etc.. Most importantly, notice the feeling of your Sacred Archetype.

Ask your Sacred Archetype to show you the perfected vision of your Soul Blueprint.

You can also ask it about a life situation that you may be dealing with. Trust your intuition and guidance.

THE I AM PRESENCE

The I Am Presence is the dimensional self also known as the individualized flame of God. The I Am Presence is the will of God that governs your reality and universal law, working through your free will. the individualized flame is the image of this divine creative presence, which is the electronic light.

Held within this electronic structure of your unique imprint of light is the Soul Blueprint. Essentially, you're like a crystalline snowflake falling to Earth, leaving its reflection on the essence of life.

As we incubate in the heart of Source Energy, we gather the momentum of consciousness to burst forth as an Individualized Flame of Light. We are here to express our gifts of love in a world of form. We have the gift of free will to know ourselves in the reflection of life.

To know one self is the conscious realization of "I Am that I Am," or in Hebrew, "Ehyeh Asher Ehyeh." This is one of the highest vibrational statements we can say because it holds within it the name of the Divine.

Within the statement "I Am that I Am", is the simplest and most profound divine truth. We as Humans are constantly, sometimes desperately searching for the answer to the question "Who am I? and What am I here for?"

Every ad you see on commercials, billboards, radio, and the internet plays on this eternal question. Telling you if you only have this product, this lifestyle, this, this or this, you will know yourself and feel whole. I'm sure you've noticed by now, it doesn't work that way.

Reverse This Question

If you simply reverse this eternal question and say, "What am I here for," then you would have the answer that humankind has sought throughout eternity. Once you have cracked the universal code to the greatest search in the Universe, you will have the Universe at your fingertips to wield the power of love throughout your life.

Therefore, instead of asking "who am I and what am I here for?" you would say "Who **I Am** and What **I Am** here for." To acknowledge and become aware of that one simple truth, "I Am" engages your innate true self.

The assumption of "I Am" is to know yourself as whole. To ask "Who am I?" engages the assumption that you don't know yourself and are therefore disconnected from Source. It's nothing more than a bad habit that has been passed down through the centuries.

Law of Resurrection

We're all always connected to Source, but at some point in our history, we started to focus more on the outer five senses instead of the sustaining power of our own mighty I Am Presence. At this point, we began to feel separate from our Source and lost in the Universe. We distorted the truth of our beingness with fear, instead of knowing ourselves as an Infinite Being with one hundred percent awareness and Free Will.

Krishna, in his wisdom, saw this change occurring, and knew only disharmony would come from it. He petitioned with the Karmic Board for the law of resurrection to be established so that humankind could be given help in learning how to stay in conscious connection with Source while in human form. The Karmic Board is comprised of the Lords of Karma, who dispense justice within our Universe. All souls must pass before the Karmic Board before and after each life time, where they receive their assignment and karmic allotment of energy to fulfill this assignment and review of their service upon completion.

Through the Keeper of the Scrolls and the Recording Angels, the Lords of Karma have access to the complete Akashic records of every soul. They determine who shall embody, as well as when and where. They assign souls to families and communities, measuring out the weights of karma that must be balanced in the scales of life. The Karmic Board, acting in divine alignment with the I Am Presence, determines when the soul has earned the right to be free from the wheel of karma / the wheel of reincarnation.

The Karmic Board consists of:

- Great Divine Director *(representing the first ray)*
- Goddess of Liberty *(second ray)*
- Ascended Lady Master Nada *(third ray)*
- Elohim Cyclopea *(fourth ray)*
- Pallas Athena, the Goddess of Truth *(fifth ray)*
- Portia, Goddess of Justice *(sixth ray)*
- Kuan Yin, the Goddess of Mercy *(seventh ray)*
- Recently Vairochana, one of the five Dhyani Buddhas, became the eighth member of the Karmic Board.

Jesus was a carrier of this flame of resurrection, bringing forth the teachings of resurrection and the wisdom that God is within all things. He would say, "Turn over any rock and **I Am** there; split any piece of wood and **I Am** there; **I Am** the resurrection and the life of perfection."

The season of spring is designed to be reflections throughout the nature kingdom. As everything comes back to life again, it reminds us of the resurrection.

Your Life Energy Force

Once you have gathered the momentum of consciousness to burst forth as an Individualized Flame of Light, you are then supplied with a source of electronic substance that bears the symbol of your life force energy. The more consciousness you hold, the stronger is your life essence.

Everything in the Universe has a signature to its vibration in the form of a symbol, a color, a feeling, a soul note, and a fragrance. For instance—Mother Mary's symbol is the dove, her color is rose, her quality essence feeling is Divine Love, her fragrance is rose, and her soul note can be found in the song Ave Maria.

Each of the ascended hosts has a signature to its vibration, as does a rock, an angel, a star, a planet, a tree, an animal, a baby, and you. This is how people can recognize each other from lifetime to lifetime or from place to place. Your vibrational signature is stored in your cellular memory.

The Law of Accountability

There is another reason why everything in the Universe is stamped with a symbol that represents it, and that is accountability. For every electron of energy you put forth in the form of a thought, feeling, action, or word, it must return to you. If you send forth a blessing to someone in your life, it will pass through you as a blessing first, then go out to the person you blessed. But it doesn't stop there. It gathers momentum, magnetizing light substances of like nature as it goes. When it is returned to you, it adds to your life's purpose.

This also happens with any negative intentions you send forth, including cuss words, which are words that curse someone or something. You and you alone are responsible for the use of the electronic energy you ordain in your world. Nobody is exempt from this law and the vibrational essence stored in the center of every electron. You want to put those electrons to good use.

The Law of Cause and Effect

Electrons are living energy sources that respond with unconditional love to your every desire. They are the building blocks of creation and have no discernment as to whether your desire is negative or positive in nature. They just want to be of service to you in any way you direct them. As the light body substance of Source Energy, they are given to you as a steward of the light to act on behalf of conscious creation. Once this electronic substance is released to you, it is entrusted to your care.

For these electrons to enter your consciousness, they must go through your energy bodies. Therefore, if you are filled with negative thoughts or feelings, these precious electrons hit the wall of this negative energy and are instantly warped to this form, almost crippling them in their potency to serve you. But in their unconditional form of love for you, they will render any service you desire.

Do you see how you are master of your world (whether you like it or not) and are responsible for all your thoughts, feelings, emotions, intentions and actions? Don't look for a shortcut to universal law. It simply is the structure of the Universe, the law of karma or cause and effect. Through every action is a reaction. This is the basis of how a soul learns to evolve through free will. We also learn from the law of karma through the reflection of your physical reality how to remember your divinity from within the veil of forgetfulness/ illusion.

This electronic substance that fills the Universe and sustains it with prana or life force energy is freely given to you for the purpose of fulfilling your Soul Blueprint. Your Soul Blueprint is an energetic code stored in the nucleus of every cell of your being and in every electron dispensed to you. It is a tiny blue flame held within an elliptical electronic light substance, also referred to as the liquid light of God.

There is no escaping your life purpose, although you may try delaying it. The Soul Blueprint is the chemistry of life that creates the matrix of infinite possibilities to express your gift of love. It magnetizes energy of like vibration to you, assisting you in delivering your gift of love.

When you're not in harmony to your own divinity, you distort this energy to be almost the exact opposite of what it was meant to be. That invokes the law of duality or cause and effect, also known as karma. This law assists you in rebalancing your life force energy to be in harmony with the laws of life.

Master Teacher

The I Am Presence is our master teacher, always acting as a blessing for the highest good of all. Each lifetime is an evolution of the fulfillment of the Soul Blueprint, building a tapestry of light that lives eternally as an expression of the Divine manifesting through you. You are both the artist and the steward of this eternal tapestry of light.

Your beloved I Am Presence has its own aura of light around it called the causal body, which is not the same aura of the emotional body. It is comprised of seven concentric circles of light, which connect to the seven chakras of the body.

This is where your Divine Inheritance is stored. Whenever you perform acts of service or evolve yourself through one of the seven laws that govern the seven chakras, that energy (when returned) is stored in this storehouse of light until you need it to fulfill your Soul Blueprint.

For instance, you may have a storehouse in the circle of Divine Wisdom from years, even lifetimes, of studying with the ascended and living masters. Perhaps in this lifetime, you are destined to write a book that would further evolve the consciousness of the individuals who read it. Or you may have rendered countless acts of unconditional service to your family and community and have a storehouse in the chakra for Divine Love. Or you may be a healer/doctor and have a storehouse in the chakra for Divine Vision and Healing. In many ways, you can build good karma through your own evolution and unconditional service to add to your storehouse of the causal body.

Form Needed for Your Soul

When this living light is released, it will come in the form most needed for your soul's use. For instance, you may think you need money. But when the light from the flame of wisdom is released into your use, it may be in the form of channeled information or a great idea that needs to be patented or written into a book. If you use this energy wisely, money comes.

If you are highly developed in the storehouse of Divine Manifestation, you may have a windfall of money come to you. Or perhaps you were even born with it so you could be of service to your destiny or those in your sphere of influence.

Only you and your I Am Presence really know what these gifts are. What is the best way to find out? Go inside and ask your I Am Presence what has been stored. At times, it can be light, love, wisdom, power, sacred objects from other lifetimes, books of wisdom, or wealth that has been reserved for you until this lifetime.

When you ask your I Am Presence to take you to your causal body, notice which ring of light is the brightest and what color it is. These colors will correlate to the universal laws that also govern the crown of light: pink, yellow, blue, white, green, violet, and ruby. Then ask to be told or shown your Divine Inheritance and how to release it. Sometimes, the release of the Divine Inheritance depends on timing or acquiring the maturity needed. I always qualify the energy with releasing it to me in the perfect timing and in the perfect way—to be governed by my I Am Presence.

Free Will

Free will is an instrument of the Divine to ignite the connection between your human consciousness and your Divine consciousness. Free will is therefore the perfect tool to use when connecting to your I Am Presence.

Don't take the gift of free will lightly. It can have a profound effect in your life when you come into alignment with it. It is the act of union with the Divine; "I will to will Thy will," which means you are consciously choosing your love for Source in each and every moment.

When you are an instrument of the light, you are capable of acting with infinite power, but you must realize the source of this infinite power of the Universe is Divine Love itself. To use your free will, choose your love for Source and all of life. This will allow you to be an instrument of "Thy" will, which is the presence of the Divine acting through you.

It is the same with your I Am Presence. This relationship requires your surrendering to be of service to a higher good than your personality and ego-based needs, which are usually fear-based and selfish. Free will means you are consciously choosing to recognize the Divine presence in yourself and others, or you are not. This is what "namaste" means: "The Divine in me honors the Divine in you."

You make choices daily, but free will is a divine act. With your free will, you can either allow the electronic substance of Light to enter your being or you can reject it. Many times in a day, your subconscious issues and unresolved emotions limit your ability to receive the electrons that have been allotted to you for this use.

You may not realize you are blocking the support you so desperately want. But regardless of your prayers, your subconscious issues can win out until they are resolved in the particular area you want help in. When you don't own the power of your Divine Right to use your free will and break the cords that bind you to discord, you negate the power of your I Am Presence to act triumphantly over any obstacle in your path.

Separation

Places you most likely are not using your free will are in areas of separation.

Ask, "What would it take for me to transmute and heal all the places I feel separate or block The Pure Love and Light of Source flowing gracefully in around and through me? Please clear anything in the way of this. I am asking the Universe to download any frequencies I need into my body to support me in my connection and wholeness with Source."

Have faith in your I Am Presence to take command of your life and bring you freedom and victory. For instance, you can say, "I am choosing my free will in this situation within my relationship today and am asking my beloved I Am Presence to take command of this situation for the highest good of all."

By choosing your free will, you are taking the higher path of your Higher consciousness instead of the "little self." Remembering the words Namaste "the Divine in me honors the Divine in you" is always a great place to start resolving conflicts of any kind.

Many times, feeling separate from our own higher consciousness comes from how we were raised and how those who raised us felt separate. As children, we tend to collapse the relationships of those that raised us onto God, thereby limiting the Divine within us to act freely. When you collapse your mental beliefs and emotional reactions of your human relationships, such as the relationship with your parents or other authority figures in your life, you are limiting the Higher Presence within you to the same human discord.

The Divine Presence is infinite and should not be subject to the limitations of our human discord. As an example, your father was not present to you as a child because of work, divorce, emotional unavailability, alcoholism, and so on; therefore, you don't believe God will be there for you when you need him most.

This is a classic example of collapsing your relationship with the disappointment about your father onto your relationship with

God. Your beliefs limit your own potential of seeing the higher truth and evolving beyond the issue of abandonment.

Go back and find these limitations. Look at your life. Are you judgmental or critical of yourself, lacking love, longing for something you do not have? This is a great place to start your inquiry.

Ask your I Am Presence to assist you in releasing anything that no longer serves your highest well-being, then let it go. Any weak links in your spiritual flow will wreak havoc until they are brought back into Divine Alignment. A weak link is usually easy to find because it registers as a complaint or unfulfilled need. It simply needs to be reconnected, which is what your I Am Presence specializes in. Just be willing to turn it over and watch the synchronicity of miracles happen.

Steward of Light

The I Am Presence knows that it is a steward of the light of divine purpose and that the physical form and consciousness is a vehicle for this service. The I Am Presence is dispensed by the electronic substance of Light to support and sustain your Divine Blueprint. It magnetizes needs to be met in every situation for the highest good of all. We must simply ask that all blocks are cleared from our path of receiving, and it is given.

The I Am Presence is the commanding part of us that knows how to govern the universal laws of co-creation. It works in harmony with all the Tribes of Light, particularly the Ascended Host. The I Am Presence sends forth the perfected vision of any situation to your Higher Self and the quality essence or feeling to your soul. It communicates through the sacred fire of the three-fold flame of love, power, and wisdom within the heart. As it does, it activates the holy trinity of the Divine within you.

Tube of Electronic White Light

The formula for having what you most desire is the activity of creating a permanent atom. In the following meditation, you magnetize the electronic substance of light through the guidance of your I Am Presence. You can command the I Am Presence to bring down, around, and through you the tube of pure electronic tube of white light.

This tube of electronic white light will literally begin to protect you from electromagnetic energy fields, (EMF) and begin raising your consciousness to a higher frequency vibration while filtering out negative thought forms and emotions that are bouncing around you in your environment and collective unconscious.

It acts as an invincible armor of Light sustaining you in your world. "I Am calling forth to my beloved I AM Presence to enfold me in the tube of pure electronic white light acting as the invincible armor of Light now; igniting within every atom of my existence the light which supplies, sustains, protects, and illumines me in the fulfillment and manifestation of my Soul Blueprint."

Permanent Atom Meditation

To begin, center yourself by focusing on your breath flowing in and out of your heart center. Notice your heartbeat. Then notice the heartbeat of the Universe. Allow these two heartbeats to come into rhythm with each other. This is known as a one-heart breath; you are connecting to your own Divine rhythm. Notice the desire within your heart. Begin to visualize the image you see. Then project this visual with your third eye into a bubble in front of you.

Next, generate within your heart center all your love, adoration, and gratitude for this desire and its outcome. Send a ray of pink light from your heart into the bubble sustaining it until it is saturated with divine love.

Next, go to your crown chakra and generate a yellow ray of Divine Wisdom that holds the Soul Blueprint for this desire. After that, send it forth as a ray of bright yellow light into the bubble in front of you until it gets saturated with color.

Next, go to your throat chakra and gather the energy of your divine will to make manifest this desire, gathering the blue ray of divine power. When you feel committed and strong, send forth a blue ray of divine power and will to put this desire into action.

Now, seal this bubble in the ruby ray of divine peace from the third chakra. Saturate the bubble with this ruby ray of light sealed in a ring of gold. This will prevent outer discord from disturbing your creation.

Imagine releasing your Permanent Atom to one or all of the following: onto the altar of the silent watcher, the Divine Mind, the Heart of All Creation, Source Energy to be blessed and organized for your highest good.

There, it will be blessed into manifested form and released to your I Am Presence to govern. Sit in your love, adoration, and gratitude that it is done. And so it is.

This is a great way to work actively with your I Am Presence, practicing co-creation and being an instrument of the Divine. It also assists you in reconnecting the weak links in your human consciousness back to your Divine consciousness.

THE COSMIC CHRIST PRESENCE

The use of the word "Christ" is referred to as a state of consciousness, and not intended to make reference to the Christian messiah known as Jesus Christ. The word "Christ" is taken from the Greek word meaning "to anoint." To anoint means to consecrate, to make sacred or holy, to devote oneself to a purpose or cause.

The word "Christ" is meant as a title of illumination and heightened consciousness. It is the regaining of one's true identity and the inheritance bequeathed by the Divine in all of us. To be Christed is to be awakened to the Divine within. Jesus was a great Master Teacher of this original teaching and therefore holds the title of Jesus the Christ. But each of us has this Holy Christed self within.

The Cosmic Christ Presence is the highest dimensional part of you that lives in the sacred heart of the Divine and never steps out of union with this Divine Source. It only knows Divine Perfection and Divine Love. The Cosmic Christ Presence is your origin of divinity from which your consciousness flows.

It is the keeper of your Soul Blueprint. It is constantly streaming forth a radiance of this Perfection, Pure Love and Light, carrying the seed of your Soul Blueprint to your I Am Presence. This Presence then streams the light of this perfected vision to your Higher Self, which in turns streams the light of the perfected feeling to your soul and activated in your light body. These five dimensional selves work in harmony with one another.

The Cosmic Christ Presence is the innate part of you. It sends forth the Pure Love and Light to sustain the essence of who you are, including the beating of your heart and every breath you take. You simply could not exist without it. It is the innate Divine consciousness that flows through every atom of your existence.

The Cosmic Christ Presence dispenses to you in the form of electrons, the electronic substance of Pure Love and Light in absolute perfection. The electronic substance is encoded with the Soul Blueprint, of which your Cosmic Christ Presence is the gatekeeper. As a result of this encoded, sustaining light, you attract to you all that is vibrating at a similar frequency to support you in your journey. With energy, like attracts like.

Know that the Cosmic Christ Presence holds the Soul Blueprint of your perfection as a steward of your perfection and grace. You are then distributed an allotted amount of energy to fulfill this destiny, and are held accountable for every ounce of it. Sometimes people use this energy wisely, sometimes they don't. This universal accounting system is upheld whether you are an

Angel, an Ascended Master, a Cosmic Being, a Human Being, or a Nature Spirit.

Energy in Balance

Remember that we all use the same source of universal light, and we are all responsible for keeping our energy bank accounts balanced. A misuse of energy (too much or too little) will have an effect in the world. Awareness and communication with our other dimensional selves can greatly assist in keeping energy in balance.

Your I Am Presence sits closest to your Cosmic Christ Presence. It is capable of delegating this energy and has the greatest understanding of how to manifest your Soul Blueprint in divine alignment. The I Am Presence is best at commanding this electronic substance in alignment with the universal laws in your reality. Your I Am Presence governs the right use of this energy. How? *You simply turn over all situations of your life daily to your I Am Presence to govern.*

Your I Am Presence then shows your Higher Self the perfected vision for what is supposed to happen—if you take time to connect to your higher vision to see the highest truth. From here, you can activate this vision with the presence of your soul through the perfected feeling.

Coming into Integrity

Often, we become so lazy in one or more of our dimensional bodies that we are reduced to acting in discordant ways and untruths that don't serve us or others. The key to reawakening them is to focus on them until we have the clarity we desire.

Sometimes this will take more effort than other times, depending on the strength of the illusions we've fallen into.

Think of it this way. When you're in alignment within yourself, you act, speak, feel, and think all the same thing, you are congruent within yourself and make compatible life choices. You live in integrity with your inner justice system. Become the watcher in your world and increase your awareness of the results in your life. Be aware of the feelings produced when you are out of alignment. Develop the act of detachment, which I have found is a remarkable process.

The first thing I do is catch myself wanting to react to something. Then I wait. I don't give into the temptation to react mindlessly. Instead, I focus on my breathing for 10 to 30 seconds to gain more awareness of the situation. As you practice this technique, you can interrupt all kinds of behavior patterns that are simply bad habits.

Most of us get out of practice with taking this much conscious responsibility for our experiences. Actually, we have been taught from an early age to discount our feelings, dreams, inspirations, and visions. So often we feel one thing but say another, or act one way but think another. It takes a little effort to re-train ourselves to the ability of inner listening so that we are in harmony to the divine inspirations, which has a Divine influence on us.

Too many times, we tend to jump to the conclusion that a Higher Presence doesn't hear us, love us, or protect us. We believe that life isn't perfect, we're not supported, and problems are perpetual in life. Perhaps none of this is true—it's just that we haven't been taught to listen, align, and act on behalf of the Divine. I believe if we listen to ourselves before acting, it could simplify the majority of accidents, problems, and disagreements in our life.

Start by learning to recognize the truth for yourself, then telling the truth to others and sustaining your actions to reflect this truth. Above all, do not break agreements with yourself. Stay focused on your commitments between you and Spirit. Don't be swayed from the inner truth that guides you.

Notice Your Awareness

As you consistently pray with your Cosmic Christ Presence and send forth love and adoration through your sacred heart, it will notice your awareness. Once this happens, your Cosmic Christ Presence will begin to enlighten you with your Soul Blueprint. It will start dispensing a greater supply of energy and resources to fulfill the destiny you were designed to co-create. Otherwise, your Cosmic Christ Presence assumes that you are unconscious and dormant, that you aren't able to act consciously and carry out the Divine Plan.

This is not a judgment; it's just a fact of energetic truth. *You can't do what you're not aware to do.* It would be like giving a child fire, the fire of creation; it takes spiritual maturity to manage such a gift.

Love Gathers Momentum

Every saint, master, and mystic at some point came to this awareness on their journey of conscious awakening. They began to develop relationships with their Cosmic Christ Presence by sending love, adoration, and gratitude to the heart of their Divine Presence. This love gathers momentum until it gets the attention of the Cosmic Christ Presence, thus releasing the flood gates of

Divine Love back into the physical world for the victory and fulfillment of Spirit's Divine Plan.

Remember, you are the steward of that Plan in the form of your Soul Blueprint, which requires you to remain consistent, strong, and determined. It also requires you to use your free will by choosing your love for Spirit in each moment.

Your Cosmic Christ Presence then sets into motion a pouring forth of the electronic light body substance of Source Energy, which will take the form of your conscious direction. It streams in, around, and through you until you are a radiant and magnetic light of pure perfection in the world of form. It constantly flows, acting as a blessing to all of life, like it has for the mystics, saints, and masters who have come before you.

Remember, *as high as you are focused is as high as you will go.*

That means if you only focus on the lower elements of energy such as problems and negative opinions, worry and fear, then that's where your consciousness will live and create your experience. But when you start to focus on the higher levels of energy within the higher elevated emotions of Love and Above energy, then you will have those experiences that will honor and bless you with the abundance of supply you are willing to accept and allow into your life.

The ability to be aware of all aspects of consciousness and dimensional selves is important to your evolutionary growth. But to know how to access the door to Source energy which only you can open or close, opens a floodgate of infinite possibilities and resources beyond your wildest imagination.

These resources cannot be generated by other aspects of consciousness. When you go to Source Energy, you release the full magnitude of the Divine Presence within you. It allows you to take compassionate action through your I Am Presence, Higher Self, Soul, and Light Body to support you in this physical dimension.

Cosmic Christ Meditation

Take a moment to begin focusing on the rhythmic flow of your breathing. Begin to notice the rhythm of your heart beat, and as you follow it to its source, to the pulsing rhythm of the Universe breathing life into your very existence. Gently allow yourself to be enfolded in the tender embrace of the emanations of the warm glowing light of your Cosmic Christ Presence, sustaining you in the heart of Creation.

Letting go of everything of the physical world, and then feeling yourself fully supported by this Divine Presence aligning your life into harmonious perfection and grace. Just resting here eternally, feeling the rejuvenation and fullness of this light bringing strength and freedom to live your life as an instrument of the Pure Love and Light of Source So it is.

Masters Meditation

Still the outer self by focusing your breath flowing through the heart. Connect to your own heartbeat and the heartbeat of the Universe, allowing them to harmonize again— usually within three to twelve breaths.

Then visualize yourself in a dazzling white light. This is your outer self. Once you have a strong image of this, keep your attention on this brilliant white light, but also focus your attention on the heart center.

Visualize it as a golden sun. Recognize and feel the connection between your outer self and Source Energy, again allowing them to pulse as one.

Then acknowledge this truth: *"I now joyously accept the Pure Love and Light and Perfection of my Cosmic Christ Presence flooding in, around and through me as a living blessing to all life."*

Continue to feel the great brilliancy and light intensify in every cell of your being for ten minutes longer.

Close your prayer with this command: *"I am a steward of the light, I love the light, I serve the light, I live in the light, I am protected, illumined, supplied, and sustained by the light, and I bless the light!"*

THE TRIBE OF LIGHT

Have you ever wondered where you were from, as if you've known all along there was more to you that meets the eye? Have you ever felt that no one seems to understand you or that you must have been adopted and that you had some other really cool family somewhere in a distant galaxy that perfectly understood the language you speak? Well, if you have ever pondered such things before, get ready to learn the truth of your origin.

Just like you have a human family and heritage, you also have a Tribe, Council, Family of Light and a Divine Heritage. Both of these families influence you in the expression of your life. Your human family supplies your soul with life lessons for your own evolution.

Often, people choose family members who play out opposites to push against in the form of karmic issues. The Family of Light assists you in fulfilling your sacred contract with spirit and in doing this They honor your sacred contract as much as you do and will do everything they can to support you in this cause. You and your Tribe of Light are essentially one; you communicate through one mind, one heart, one touch.

Family on this Earth

Karma deals with the laws of duality—which is learning from action and reaction so we return to the middle path, the law of one. The heritage from our human family affecting us at a subconscious level is based on lineage patterns coming from parents, grandparents, great grandparents, and so on. The majority of these patterns get "downloaded" into our unconscious in the womb, which is preverbal. They get confirmed in reality when we're born and live within the constructs of these lineage patterns.

Most children carry greater evolutionary resources than their parents because they have just returned from spirit. That's where they were integrating their last human experience and the wisdom gained from life experiences. Therefore, children in each generation are committed to evolve the unconscious issues of the last generation to the next level of self realization— and to the remembrance of our Soul Blueprint.

On average, a human soul rests in spirit form, usually in the Temples of Light with their Tribe of Light for one hundred to one thousand years before re-entering another body. This allows time to assimilate all the experiences of the last life. Sometimes a soul will rush this natural timing and come back more quickly. At this time on Earth, many souls have done this for the purpose of contributing to the ascension of Earth and the family of humanity.

However, there can be a price paid for returning so quickly. It can come in such forms as a weakened nervous system, immune system, oversensitivity, stress, anxiety, and chronic fatigue. If you feel like this, it may be an issue for you. Make sure you counterbalance this with preventive nutrition, sleep, meditation, and water. Call forth your Tribe of Light to take you into sacred healing chambers to rejuvenate you while you sleep.

Tribe of Light

I'd like you to imagine that we all come from a universal source. We have a gift of love that we wish to bring forth on behalf of our Divine Presence as a steward of creation. As we step out of this light, we become an individualized flame of God, also known as the I Am Presence. We start traveling through the dimensions of consciousness and begin to merge with one of the seven basic Tribes of Light so we can develop the wisdom, gifts, and tools necessary to deliver this gift of love on behalf of the Divine. It's like having an adjustment period before entering into physical form.

The seven basic Tribes of Light within this universal system include: Cosmic Avatars, Galactic Counsels, Planetary Light Beings, Star Tribes, Angelic Hierarchy, Ascended Masters, and Nature Kingdom. All of these Tribes of Light offer these basic services:

1. They assist you in fulfilling your Soul Blueprint, which is between you and Source.

2. They assist you in your heart's desires, which are between you and your soul, and are relevant to your daily needs.

3. They fund energy into your prayers, blessings, decrees and intentions.

4. They enfold you in quality essences, such as love, faith, wisdom, strength. They take you into sacred healing chambers of light for healing in all four bodies (physical, etheric, emotional, and mental). This includes inner learning schools and Temples of Light to better train you in your gifts.

5. Finally, they go before you and create a synchronicity of miracles in your life. By aligning all the right people, places, timing of events, and so on.

Your Tribe of Light assists you through dharma instead of karma. Dharma is your ability to be of service through the unconditional offering of the wisdom gained from your life lessons learned and the gifts of love evolved from your soul's journey. Your Tribe of Light is not perceived as opposite of your true nature, but rather *one* with your true nature.

Other members of your Tribe of Light can enter into human form as well. If you are fortunate enough to ever have this occurrence, it's like experiencing another part of your own soul. It's amazing to feel so understood and similar to someone else on your soul journey. The members of your Tribe of Light know your true purpose and intentions; they are supportive and are always by your side. In knowing your Tribe of Light, you know that you are never alone in this world. They are comforting, peaceful, and full of wisdom and healing light.

You may be asking, "If these Beings are so great and always by my side, then why haven't I ever seen them or known about them before?" Well, have you ever seen little babies looking around a room and you can tell they're watching something, but you just can't tell what? Or your pets go crazy when you meditate or do healing work? It's the same thing. Babies and animals have a highly developed etheric vision, meaning they can see energy, lights, and colors better than they can see physical reality. Babies are mostly watching their own Tribe of Light and those of others.

Most babies are still connected to their Divine Presence instead of the outer five senses. Between age two and five, they get trained to focus on the world around them instead of the inner realms. On some level, this is appropriate, because everyone is on Earth to deliver gifts of love, but it is unfortunate that children aren't taught to maintain a connection to both worlds.

Your Tribe of Light assists you in the birthing process and the death process, too. When you leave this world, members of your Tribe of Light greet you and assist you with that transition. They take you back into the Temples of Light where you came from. They help you integrate that lifetime and understand the wisdom gained, so you can return more "whole" and with greater strength to fulfill your Soul Blueprint.

When you get ready to come back in to form again, they enfold you in a cocoon of light while your body is growing in the womb, continuing to teach you about the soul gifts required to support you in that life time. They assist you in the birthing process and remain with you on the inner levels until you are complete with your life path.

Those in your Tribe of Light are Master Teachers who welcomed you into their world and began teaching you what you would need to know in fulfilling your Soul Blueprint. These Master Teachers hold great wisdom and love within their hearts. They are committed out of their love for you to help you develop your strengths and skills as an instrument of the Divine They have watched you grow in each and every lifetime, and know the truth of who you are better than anyone. The love between them and you is immeasurable and unconditional. Leaving the comfort of their presence may not have been the easiest thing to do when it was time to be born into the world. But those in your Tribe of Light taught you well and blessed your journey with their faith in your gift of love to be bestowed upon the family of humanity.

Look to Your Tribe of Light

I'd like to help you remember the ancient history of wisdom of your Divine Heritage and the love your Tribe of Light has never ceased guiding you with, like the north star in the sky above. All you have to do is look up to see their lights shining down upon you.

Once you have reconnected to the Beings in your Tribe of Light, you will begin to feel their presence and all the gifts they bestow upon you in human form. As your personal assistants and guidance counselors, they enfold you in quality essences such as love, faith, hope, love, courage. They assist you in fulfilling your heart's desires, prayers, and blessings. They are like worker bees that will go out on your behalf and align the perfect people, opportunities, and timing of events to support you. They fund energy to you and through you into your world, creating a synchronicity of miracles in your daily life. This allows your life to flow in harmonious perfection and alignment toward reaching your Soul Blueprint.

There is only one catch; *you have to invite them in to be of service with you.* So start by treating them like your new best friends; the more you call them in, the better you get to know them. As loving and magical as these Beings are, they cannot cross the boundaries of your free will. Honestly, I feel they would do a much better job than most of us do managing our lives, but that's not the way it works.

Through prayers and blessings, you can request them to come forth and assist. It's like picking up a phone and making a collect call to heaven. If you never pick up the phone, no call is made therefore no help answers. You will begin to realize that you're not alone in this world— and perhaps never have been. It's a huge relief to know you don't have to figure everything out and fix the whole world just to feel safe and happy in it!

Praying with the Tribe of Light

All people have a Tribe, Family, Council of Light that watches over them and hears their prayers while assisting them on their life paths. Whether or not you know which Tribe of Light you or another belongs to, you can simply use the code word "Tribe, council, or family of Light" in your prayers when you want specific assistance, either for yourself or another person or group. When making the call to the Tribe of Light on behalf of another you can be at peace knowing that you have not crossed someone's boundary because every soul has the right to refuse the blessing or let it in with the use of free will. Most people don't reject the prayer; they simply forget to say it for themselves. Or they don't know how to do it.

For instance, you can pray for your partner's and your children's Tribe of Light to come forth and assist them for their highest good for a meeting, a trip, a health or safety issue, a test, or even happiness. The Tribe of Light will show up on their behalf and fund energy to the prayer request you made. If your prayer doesn't serve the highest well-being for them, or the help just isn't wanted, the soul will refuse the energy. Your prayers will still be a blessing in their lives.

No request is too small or too big—from finding a parking space to fulfilling your Soul Blueprint. The more specific you are in your requests, the more specific the results. For instance, you can ask for support in a meeting, or on a trip, for good weather, a relationship issue, or a financial concern.

If you don't know what to ask them for assistance with, then ask them to align your day in harmonious perfection, divine alignment, a synchronicity of miracles, or any other quality you'd like to experience. Your Tribe of Light actually evolves through getting to be of service with you, so don't worry that you're asking for too much. You just have to play with them. I guarantee your inner child loves them already, and will instantly recognize and respond to them as the magical beings they are.

In the morning, I would recommend calling forth Tribe of Light to ordain your day as previously recommended. At night before going to bed or if you're not feeling well, ask your Tribe of Light to place you in a sacred healing chamber. Treat them as if they're your own personal spirit doctors. They know how to balance your physical, mental, emotional, and spiritual bodies, rejuvenate and heal you. In the sacred healing chamber, they will initiate a graceful healing process. Their loving presence feels like a warm blanket softly enfolding you. It creates a deep level of safety, allowing your feelings to rise from the depths to the surface, which can be the healing you most need at times.

You can also ask them at night before going to sleep or while meditating to take you into Temples of Light. Within the Temples of Light, you can gain the wisdom of your soul gifts, life purpose, divine partnership, flow of abundance and resources, conflict resolutions to life issues you are having, and much more.

You may experience these temples as a lucid dream or a profound realization upon waking. You may simply notice that you're thinking differently or that after several weeks, things will go your way again. Stay open to their service with you; it can be direct or subtle, but they will assist you whether you can see them or not. They will always work with maximum efficiency, and minimum effort. And they'll help you do the same.

Remembering Your Tribe of Light

Do you remember seeing your Tribe of Light as a child? It's funny to see how people don't believe they have a Tribe of Light at first. Either it sounds too good to be true, or everyone *except them* will be able to connect with their Tribe of Light. But it doesn't take much to jog their memories. All of a sudden, they recall the night when, as a child, they saw a Being of Light by their bedsides.

They didn't know what it was when they heard voices talking to them or saw flashes of light out the corners of their eyes. Perhaps once or twice they remembered encounters when the veil between worlds was thin. But the memory touched them so deeply that they can still recall it years later when they give themselves the chance.

Visions, Superheroes, and the Tribe of Light

Take a minute to feel if there are any memories or visions you've forgotten, or tucked away somewhere to keep safe. Allow yourself to remember that feeling you had when you *knew* a loving presence was watching over you.

As for me, I had three imaginary friends, Herman, Dobbin, and Rubin. I don't remember much about them except they kept me company and seemed really fun. My mother remembers them a little differently; she said I used to blame everything mischievous on them. I guess I figured they might as well help any way they could!

It has always amazed me how we live a double life between our sleeping dream and waking dream. It's like living in two parallel Universes, crossing without remembrance from one world into the other. It reminds me of superheroes who do magnificent feats of service, but once they take off their costumes, they seem normal and can't even imagine themselves being courageous.

And then one day, their inner and outer worlds collide in the space-time continuum. They feel like they've have been struck by lightning. All of a sudden, they realize they don't need a mask to separate their worlds any longer. They become their soul's magnificence— in service with a whole team of universal superheroes called their Tribe of Light to assist them.

If you're curious about which Tribe of Light is working on your behalf, a free quiz and resource guide can be found at www. mywildmagic.com.

Tribe of Light Meditation

To begin connecting to your original Tribe of Light, start by breathing deeply into your heart center.

You may want to close your eyes to expand your inner vision. Use your intuition to sense, see, feel or know your Tribe of Light.

When you feel centered, call forth to your Tribe of Light to come in and around you.

Notice the first color frequencies that begin to come towards you that are representing your Tribe of Light.

Then notice the feeling of these Beings as they enfold you in their light. Is it warm, loving, vibrant, or perhaps calming?

Ask your Tribe of Light to reveal themselves to you in energetic form.

Ask if they are cosmic, galactic, planetary, star, angelic, ascended master, or nature beings. Ask them to take you into the Temples of Light that you are from and reveal to you the soul gifts and purpose of your life.

COSMIC TRIBE OF LIGHT

The Cosmic Beings are the rarest of the seven Tribes of Light. They hold such an expanded universal consciousness it can seem as if they don't really relate to this world at times. They can also be aloof and like being alone or in nature over any of the mundane activities of most human beings. They are able to meditate and go very far out into the Universes. These people are usually souls who come from far away to be on Earth.

They are gifted at seeing beyond the illusion of separation, time and space. Cosmic Avatars understand the truth of the Law of Divine Love and Oneness so well that they are not bound to time, space, death, and other Earthly phenomena. They love by and know instinctually the higher laws of the Universe and teach them to those they feel can expand their consciousness to receive the information. Eckhardt Tolle is a good example of a modern-day Cosmic Avatar.

The Cosmic Beings are the rarest of the seven Tribes of Light. They hold such an expanded universal consciousness that we don't even recognize their existence most of the time. It's like a fish in the ocean that doesn't realize it's in an ocean until it's taken out of the water.

These Beings are able to create planetary systems with their divine love and consciousness. People who work with Cosmic Beings are able to respond to the consciousness of these Beings. These people are usually souls who come from far away to be on Earth.

Cosmic Beings—and the souls that register to their frequency of energy—have the signature of living purely within the Law of Divine Love. They teach this Law of Divine Love and Oneness in its pure form to the family of humanity in a loving, graceful, and detached way. Beings representing this Tribe of Light are often referred to as Cosmic Avatars.

Gifted at unveiling the illusion of time and space, these Cosmic Avatars understand the truth of the Law of Divine Timing

They know how to live beyond the boundaries of illusion and separation. Every couple thousand years, one of these Cosmic Avatars—with great consciousness—steps forth into our world to remind us of what's possible beyond the fish bowl of our limited humanity.

When Cosmic Avatars are finished introducing the frequency of energy they wished to contribute to the family of humanity, they can leave at will. That means they can raise their consciousness into the light and enter into another dimensional frequency. Cosmic Avatars know there is no such thing as death; therefore, they're not bound to the karmic wheel of life and death or some of the other concepts we believe in.

Some of the other assumptions that we as humans make, but Cosmic Beings do not include the laws of gravity, time, and space. They are able to teleport as well as be at different places at the same time. They are able to manifest at will because they understand the source of creation and the laws that govern it. Some of the stories relating to the Cosmic Beings have been documented throughout time, such as the life of Babaji, Tibetans, and yogis who live to be five hundred years old, and the stories of Baird Spalding in his journeys throughout the far east where he met with living and Ascended Masters.

A Gift to the Earth Itself

Among the gifts these Divine Beings bring forth is a gift to the Earth itself. Their consciousness is so high that it acts as an acupuncture point of light in the Earth's electrical field thus helping raise the Earth's energy level for her ascension. These beloved Beings are conscious of the higher service they render on Earth. It goes beyond the journey of self. They have already developed the love to fulfill their teachings.

To connect to these awesome Beings—because you feel they are your Tribe of Light or just because you want to sit in their resonance—imagine sitting in the expanded consciousness of your own Cosmic Christ Presence. This will begin to expand your Cosmic Christ Presence in physical form to blaze forth into your life path and ignite your Soul Blueprint.

Remember, every conscious being has a creative ray of light that governs its existence as a steward of the light of Source. You are an individualized flame of God. The creative ray is the essence of your own Cosmic Christ Presence. The creative ray holds a signature of light and sound frequencies unique to you.

Held within this creative ray of light is the impression of the Soul Blueprint that you are meant to fulfill. It is called a creative ray instead of an Earth ray or universal ray because it implies an act of co-creation, which is what conscious beings are designed to do. You can use your life force energy to support another conscious being's creative ray—such as the creative ray of Jesus in the principles of his teachings, or the creative ray of Kwan Yin, Buddha, St. Germain, or any other being you resonate with. Even the Ascended Host offers light to other Ascended Beings to assist in strengthening their creative rays. For instance, many of the members of the Ascended Host support St. Germain in his creative flame of freedom through the Violet Transmuting Flame.

Gaining Strength

As a student of the light, when you consciously act to support another being's creative flame you have an opportunity to gain strength in the area of consciousness in which that being is highly developed. It can assist you in building character, awareness, and attributes that will strengthen your will and fulfill your own creative ray.

In human form, you see this happening with parent and child, teacher and student, leader and follower; it's a natural way of evolving your own life path. But keep in mind you will eventually have to step into an expression of your own creative ray and Divine Blueprint. Your Soul Blueprint is a sacred contract between you and the heart of Creation.

The Cosmic Tribe of Light and your own Cosmic Christ Presence can assist you in the highest teachings possible for your soul's magnificence. Sitting in their resonance awakens a magnitude of energy that will have a more perfected, balanced, and far-reaching resonance than those in human form. Even though you can have great mentors in other humans, you usually discover limitations in them eventually. At this point, it's important to go inward to pursue your own quest. That is one of the beauties of life— it always spirals back into itself so you can never get too lost on your journey. *Wherever you go, there you are.*

Constant Creation

The cosmos is infinite and eternal, filled with ancient beings, Universes upon Universes, and sparks of light constantly coming into creation. While Cosmic Beings are creating Universes, galaxies, suns, planets, stars, and moons-humans are creating babies, gardens, structures, and technologies. In the end, it's all the same, just vibrating at different frequencies of mastery. You are learning how to be a co-creator, so who better to learn from than the master creators of our Universe known as the Cosmic Beings? Alpha and Omega are Cosmic Beings of the Universe. Helios and Vesta are the Cosmic Beings that create our physical sun. Through their light, they are the life givers of our Universe. Each planet, star system, and moon has a Cosmic Being that sustains a consciousness which in turn affect us through astrological influences, just as your consciousness affects your community.

Understanding Cosmic Beings

To understand Cosmic Beings, first expand your consciousness to the infinite possibilities of the Universe— beyond what your mind knows or is even willing to except. Your mind is limited to your past and the collective unconscious. The Cosmic Beings live beyond these boundaries. In our stories of ancient mythologies, we can glimpse an idea of what it may be like to relate to Cosmic Beings such as the mythologies of the sun gods – Zeus and the All Powerful Gods that govern the celestial heavens.

The Cosmic Beings are often related to the Karmic Boards and Lords that sustain the universal laws. Because these Cosmic Beings create our worlds, they are also part of the governing presence of the Spiritual Hierarchy that is supporting the divine evolution of these worlds. On the inner levels, the Cosmic Beings may look like pure radiations of light without a definite form. They communicate to you through a sense of heightened conscious awareness and complete thoughts of a higher truth—not so much in feelings, emotions, and individual concepts, but whole truths—the big picture all at one time. It often takes a person year's and even lifetimes to decipher these forms of communication and act on them.

Most of us have not accessed the potential of our brains working in a whole brain capacity. Dolphins are examples of whole brain beings on our planet. So are the yogis who have a series of studies that can open up this state of consciousness in certain forms of meditation. If we follow the success of the yogis, then we learn that entering into whole brain activity requires detachment from the world of form—to learn to be *in* this world but not *of* it.

Being in this state allows us to enter that sacred point right in the middle of the brain and control the butterfly switch that governs the activity of the brain itself. You know that you are *not* your feelings, your thoughts, or your body. You are the governing consciousness of them. You must learn to know yourself as an aspect of conscious living light, not form. If you did, then death, time, gravity, limitation, disease, poverty, and illusions could not exist.

You cannot serve two Gods. There is only ever the Law of One, and we are all connected to one source. The negative or fear-based concepts of humanity are funded in separation and this leads us to the false concept of serving two Gods, which doesn't really exist.

Our own disassociate personality becomes the false prophet of our life path. We are always the master of our free will, and can choose our love for Source in any moment to reconnect our consciousness back to our divine source, the Law of One and the ability to manifest heaven on Earth as a being of co-creation.

When you engage with the Cosmic Beings in this way, it can change your evolutionary path and original destiny, causing a spiritual quickening to occur. Send forth your adoration, love, and gratitude to these magnificent beings and continue to integrate your consciousness with them by sitting in the resonance of their love and oneness.

Examples of modern-day souls who relate to the Cosmic Avatar Tribe of Light are:

- Eckhardt Tolle
- the Dali Lama
- Yogananda
- Babaji

- Deepak Chopra
- Sadguru
- Guru Maya
- Thicht Naht Hahn
- Ghandi
- John of God

Meditation

To connect with the Cosmic Tribe of Light, begin by focusing on your breath flowing in and out of your heart center. Allow yourself to experience your love, adoration, and gratitude for your Cosmic Christ Presence. Notice the Pure liquid light and Love of Source ebbing and flowing through every cell of your being.

It pulses to the beat of the eternal sunrise, expanding your energy field and consciousness until you feel the radiance of your love shining out in all directions. Call forth your Cosmic Christ Presence to enfold you and guide you as you return every atom of your existence back to the heart of your Cosmic Christ Presence.

You will be re-qualified in the All-Consuming Flame of Divine Love within the sacred heart. As you merge into the oneness of your Cosmic Christ Presence, ask to expand with the Cosmic Beings of Light. Once you feel like you are there, ask them to show you how you can be of highest service with your time on Earth.

GALACTIC TRIBE OF LIGHT

Galactic Beings are gifted at manifestation and creation. On the inner levels, they appear as Fire Angels and communicate by inspiring the heart. They base their service on compassionate action. Souls connected to this Tribe of Light usually have a fiery nature and are action oriented. Using their ability to do ten things at once, they are excellent at organizing an event or group of people for a higher goal.

These souls can be highly direct in their communication and they like to finish things now, not later. They care immensely and don't understand why others don't care enough. Although, they have a tendency to bowl others over with their energy, it's always out of compassion. Devoted to the cause they feel committed to, they inspire others to join them in being of service for a higher good that also serves the whole.

The Galactic Beings' consciousness dwells mostly within a place known as the Great Central Sun, which is the sun behind Earth's sun and is considered to be the central hub of our Universe. They can also come from other galaxy centers such as the Andromeda Galaxy. The Great Central Sun is a golden city of lights that hosts many different Beings of Light and Temples of Light or inner learning schools. If you are visual in your meditation, you'll probably enjoy the stunning beauty and light the Great Central Sun offers.

All systems rotate around the Great Central Sun, which radiates at a higher frequency of light than all the celestial systems, including our sun. This light activates evolution within the universal systems it radiates out to. Known as the "White Fire of God," it's the pure electronic light substance from which all life is created.

This conscious living light spirals out and back in on itself in a self-sustaining cycle as it promotes expansion in the Universe. Astrologically our Earth is currently coming into a right angle with the Great Central Sun. When this happens, the dispensation of light being directed toward the Earth is immense and will always cause a quickening within the cells, consciousness, and evolution of a planet and its inhabitants. This acceleration process can cause Earth changes, mass exodus of souls who are complete, and new souls to come forth to fund the paradigm shift that is under way.

Music of the Spheres

All of the planets, suns, moons, and stars have a rhythmic cycle in which they spin in conjunction with the Great Central Sun. Each of these celestial spheres creates a musical note, coming together to form a spatial symphony in the Universe. This harmonic resonance—called the Music of the Spheres—is the basis of all creation holding itself in form, as in "first there was sound, then light."

Because sound is the origin of all creation, disturbing these sacred frequencies and their dependency on one another can cause destruction on many levels, just as sound frequencies can be destructive within our bodies. Each of our chakras resonates to a sound. We even have what's called a soul note—the signature sound of our personal being—that comes from our sacred heart. When the chakras—or soul note—get out of harmony for humans, dis-ease and chaos follow. The celestial spheres are no different.

Mayans and the Great Central Sun

The Mayans were gifted students of the galactic rhythms of the Universe. They were the first to discover that this process of alignment takes 25,765 years to make a complete cycle. The majority of their culture and myths involved the Great Central Sun and the sun gods they worshipped.

When our Earth enters into this astrological alignment, it causes a quickening, awakening, and enlightenment within the spectrum it touches. When we enter into this photon belt of living light, it can cause everything from Earth changes to golden ages. The photon belt is a band of intense light that is near Earth at this time. A photon is a quantum of light, or the smallest particle of light at a given wave length.

It is emitted by an atom during a transition of one energy state to another. This quantum of light is a carrier of an electromagnetic field. Photon is Greek for the light or "phos." Photons travel at the speed of light and can be either a wave or a particle. Therefore, the Photon Belt is a mass of pure energy that has an immense power of creation stored in it to enfold an entire planet in its ascension.

The Mayans predicted this total alignment will take place in the year 2012. This date ends their calendar system, implying a new and unknown age will come into existence. Some refer to this paradigm shift as "a thousand years of peace."

Galactic Council

As great organizers of groups for a higher purpose, the Galactic Beings saw a need to create and sponsor the Galactic Council within the hub of the Universe, the Great Central Sun. The Galactic Council is a collective group of Beings who govern the spiritual court system in our Universe. It includes a multitude of different Beings—Cosmic Beings, Angelic Beings, Planetary Beings, Star Beings, and Ascended Masters—who unconditionally agreed to be of service within the Council.

Their mission is to assist in the ascension of the Earth and the family of humanity's evolution, as well as support any planetary system in need. So, there are true Galactic Beings originating from the Great Central Sun or another galaxy center who are seen as Fire Angels of creation.

Then there are Beings of Light whose origin is from another Family of Light. They have chosen to be in service to the Galactic Councils. To clarify this point, you or another soul may be in service to a Galactic Council, but not necessarily be from the Galactic Tribe of Light.

The Galactic counsels have watched over the family of humanity since the dawn of our existence. Their interactivity with us has increased as we enter into a time period of great transition. Their presence with us has also increased as we have gained access to more powerful technologies that could destroy us and the harmonization of the Earth in the process.

To assist planets and their inhabitants to have a more graceful transition in their evolutionary process, the Galactic Council was created. (A Galactic Counsel is similar to the one depicted in the television series *Star Trek, The Next Generation, or Star Wars*.)

Send Light and Love

The Galactic Beings and Galactic Council interact with us by sending tremendous amounts of light and love. Their loving focus helps raise our vibrations and consciousness from the heart of the Great Central Sun. They govern the portals, black holes, wormholes, gateways, and super space highways to make sure beings of different natures don't override the free will of another planetary species or destroy life systems.

They guide those willing to be inspired and opened through their prayers and intention to be of service at a higher level. With this guidance, when they see an injustice in the world, they have the courage to challenge it on behalf of the well-being of the whole.

Other galaxies have a function similar to the Great Central Sun. These galaxies also act as cities of stars and host different galactic councils in their region. The Andromeda galaxy is an example. Constellations within these galaxies act as inter-dimensional hubs, and have greater concentrations of light, thus attracting many different types of dimensional space travelers. For us, it would be like being in international cities such as New York, Los Angeles, Tokyo, Sidney, or London, where the lights never go out and new trends are generated.

These souls are passionate about their message and compassionate about the lives they're inspired to touch. They won't give up their principles for anything, even if everyone has abandoned them or the cause, or they know death awaits them. These beings stand for change when no one else will.

Focus on Your Heart's Truth

We all have gifts of love to offer or we wouldn't be here on Earth. Even when we attempt doing something to the best of our ability it may look clumsy through the filter of our subconscious patterns but it's better than not trying at all. As we live and learn on this journey of life, judging our fellow brothers and sisters for their expression usually indicates not having the courage to show up in your own soul's magnificence.

The message you offer is only as clear as the clarity of its messenger. If you'd like your expression to be as pure as possible, stay focused on only the highest truth within your heart. Ask the assistance of your I Am Presence and the Galactic Tribe of Light to guide you in your divine intention and compassionate action, instead of allowing your personality and past to dictate your actions.

The Galactic Tribe of Light responds to the true heart's desire of a soul who has the highest good of all in mind and can courageously deliver the compassionate action of their soul's magnificence. Because these beings are action-oriented, you need to be committed and willing to take-action if you call them forth to assist you.

When Beings in the Galactic Tribe of Light back your cause, they send forth a great voltage of electronic light from the magnificent storehouse within the Great Central Sun to fund the success of your heart's desire. The expanded light they send forth magnetizes to you the resources needed to fulfill the desired result of your compassionate action. This is far more than you alone could do.

Galactic Champions

These Beings work fast and furiously to create miraculous outcomes in situations that could otherwise be overwhelming, hopeless, and chaotic. They champion the underdogs who have their heart in the right place. They work best in group projects that require organization to benefit a great many souls.

The Galactic Beings also referred to as the Great Central Sun Angels or Galactic Fire Angels. They specialize in manifestation. They understand the universal principles of co-creation and magnetism with the electronic light force of the Universe, which is the essence of Divine Love. They are the living hosts of the Great Central Sun, the sustainer of light within our Universe, carrying this powerfully charged light everywhere they go. Those who belong to the Galactic Tribe of Light boldly step forward to engage in revolutions of light that encourage positive change, freedom, divine rights, and evolutionary success - whether they're in the form of art, community projects, corporations, politics, revolutions, or global movements for positive change.

Example of a modern-day souls who relate to the Galactic Council Tribe of Light are:

- Oprah Winfrey
- Joan of Arc
- Jennifer Lawrence
- Matt Damon
- Martin Luther King Jr.
- Shirley MacLaine
- Brene Brown
- Esther Hicks
- Toni Robbins
- Miley Cyrus
- Bette Midler

Meditation

If you resonate with the Galactic Tribe of Light, connect with them by focusing your awareness in your heart. Then watch your heart expand like a golden sun. When you're ready, ask your Higher Self to connect you to the heart of the Great Central Sun where you would meet with the Galactic Councils, Great Central Sun Angels, and Galactic Tribe of Light. You will have a specific group of beings or Council who work with you. These Beings can help you bring about win/win solutions, give you guidance on your destiny, coach you in life choices, fund you energy to fulfill your heart's desires, and enfold you in quality essences to support your soul's magnificence.

THE PLANETARY TRIBE OF LIGHT

The Planetary Beings tend to be highly evolved and mentally superior, similar to Mr. Spock on *Star Trek*. On the inner levels, Planetary Beings can often look like beautiful tall rays of light, although sometimes you might see them as part of a planetary species found in the "Star Wars" bar scene. The Planetary Beings communicate mostly through telepathy in the mental body, the Higher Mental Body and through the Higher Self.

They teach us social responsibility and how to live as comic units in harmony with the higher good. Because of their highly developed mental bodies, they are capable of seeing the perfected vision and all the steps needed to accomplish a goal. This also gives them the ability to see all sides of a situation, which makes them great diplomats for peaceful resolutions.

The difference between the mental body and Higher Mental Body is that the mental body is often governed by your personality, your past, and your unresolved issues that your mind uses to create protective behavior patterns in your world. The Higher Mental Body sees life from a perfected vision of the mind of God. It is not limited to the past, but rather accesses the field of all possibilities. It doesn't create protective behavior patterns to limit you, but instead stands for the highest good of all that is concerned. The mind tends to be judgmental and critical; the Higher Mental Body is detached and compassionate.

The Planetary Beings have seen many different species of life go through their evolutionary processes and have become skilled at knowing what works and what doesn't— from healing the physical body, to computer science, to space travel. They offer us the wisdom of understanding the science of our own evolutionary path; they are gifted healers with light rays and DNA encoding.

Mind-Focused, Wise, and Practical

Souls that align with this Tribe of Light have an extraordinary ability to focus the mind and create their reality through mental pictures and thought forms. They also have a unique wisdom that allows them to understand deep philosophical concepts, such as quantum physics and the nature of how the Universe works. Their minds have the ability to be expanded and grounded at the same time, allowing them to solve difficult problems by reducing them to simple equations that create efficient solutions.

These stable beings are practical and logical in their approach to life. They are right about things far more than they are wrong, so if you argue with them, make sure you don't bet a lot of money. These beings often choose professions in healing, counseling, diplomacy, technology, science, philosophy, and teaching.

Quite honestly, the Planetary Beings tend to be perfectionists at anything they apply themselves to and always want the most efficient or best tools to do the job. They are very patient at staying focused, until they know what they have been working on is just right, and will refuse to be rushed. Whereas star beings, who have similar talents, are exceptionally impatient and go as fast as possible with the most technological advanced tools they can find.

Souls that come from this Tribe of Light do not like getting into emotional drama; they think it's a waste of energy. They don't speak through emotions, but are deeply compassionate. They like their "space" and prefer an orderly environment. They don't let their emotions throw them off balance and they always seek a peaceful resolution. Most people who are emotionally oriented want others to empathize with them.

These Planetary Beings are not emotionally empathetic by nature, but are compassionate. They can deeply understand you and provide resources that assist you in having clarity to make a situation better— particularly if you're not stuck or crying over spilt milk and staying attached to the emotions of the dilemma.

People who resonate with the Planetary Beings need to develop compassion to be well rounded and not just live in their heads. Emotional people need to listen to their Higher Self and use their common sense instead of always reacting emotionally. Making small adjustments like this can save a relationship. People who are emotionally based are usually kinesthetic, meaning they process information through touch and their nervous system, which is the super highway of the emotions. Touch is grounding and creates safety for those people who process through feelings. People who are mentally based process information through their Higher Mental Bodies and thought forms. So when emotional people communicate from their Higher Self by focusing attention there, they are tuning their radio to the right frequency for the Planetary Beings. This gives them a feeling of safety to understand from their Higher Self first. Planetary Beings usually prefer to understand and feel understood before being touched. The safer and more understood a Planetary Being feels, the more compassionate they are in relationship.

If you are an emotionally oriented person who is in relationship with souls from this heritage, I suggest you learn to communicate with them directly from your Higher Self to theirs. If you are from the Planetary Tribe of Light, you need to learn to gently touch emotionally based people when talking to them so they can feel valued and heard. Otherwise, two different languages are being spoken.

Emotionally and mentally oriented people are often attracted to each other because they are learning to balance their soul attributes. Souls that come from the Tribes of Light from the Angels, Star Beings, and Nature Beings are typically emotionally based. Souls that come from the Tribes of Light of the Planetary, Cosmic, and Ascended Masters are typically mentally based. The Galactic Tribe of Light is sensitive to both the emotional and mental bodies.

Channel Rays of Light

Many healers work with the Planetary Beings who have an innate understanding for light and color healing. No matter what form of healing they use such as chiropractic, teaching, or medicinal, they channel rays of light through their hands, hearts, minds, and higher consciousness, whether or not they are aware of it. This light innately flows through them to help re-balance the physical and etheric bodies.

Planetary healers have a deep understanding of the genetic make-up of the physical body, especially the expansion of a person's DNA. In science, the unused DNA, which is the majority of it, is considered junk DNA. However, this is far from the truth. New evidence shows that unused DNA can actually give us superhuman qualities of telepathy, an uncompromised immune system, the ability to touch and heal instantly, the quality of compassion, and the wisdom to understand the workings of the Universe.

Essentially, our DNA stores the makings of a living saint. This is where our evolution is leading us to—from a third-dimensional reality into the higher dimensional realities where the rules change immensely. The change has already begun, and the Planetary Beings are our guides on this exciting journey of expansion beyond the limitations of the world as we know it.

For example, scientists have recently discovered a pattern in our Milky Way that is the exact replica of a double helix found in our DNA. This provides an amazing confirmation of the sacred geometry in which all life is based. It's theorized that the planets are actually atomic structures or chakra centers comprising the body of a Cosmic Being. As the Cosmic Being evolves, humans are evolving with it as part of its body structure.

The Atlanteans, Egyptians, and others were Planetary Beings who assisted the Earth in its development by laying a foundation of crystals and gem stones for the electrical grid of the planet. The Ancient Egyptian culture was influenced by Planetary Beings. The Planetary Beings, Hathors and Arcturians trained some of the best priestesses in history, developing their minds and intuitions to manifest at high levels. The result was the construction of the Egyptian pyramids. The same is true of the Incan and Roman civilizations.

Each of our planetary systems represents planetary beings: Mercury, Mars, Venus, Saturn, Jupiter, Neptune, Uranus, Pluto, and Chiron. These are the systems closest to Earth, but other planetary systems exist beyond what we can identify, including the Arcturians. The Belt of the Orion constellation is a gateway into other systems from where the Arcturians (and some of the planetary systems) that influenced the Egyptians came from. You can find a list of the different systems in the section on Galactic, Planetary, Star System Guide on page 128.

The Planetary Beings represent the qualities and gifts of conscious evolution from whatever system they have come from. You may ask why we can't see Beings and civilizations on these other planets. It's a matter of vibrational resonance.

We believe in angels, God, Saints, Ascended masters, fairies, tree spirits, love, past lives, quantum physics and many other things that we may not be able to physically see or prove, but they clearly exist. It's a matter of vibrational resonance being different and existing in different dimensions.

We live in worlds within worlds, where the fabric of time and space overlap in fields of consciousness. For those brave enough to experience this terrain, the rewards can bring immense freedom and peace.

Examples of modern-day souls who relate to the Planetary Being Tribe of Light are:

- Albert Einstein
- Bill Gates
- David Hawkins
- Greg Bradden
- Steve Jobs
- Elon Musk
- Lynne Twist
- Abe Lincoln
- Barack Obama
- Nelson Mandela
- Dr. Christiane Northrup
- Rachel Maddow
- Nikola Tesla

Meditation

If you resonate to the Planetary Beings Family of Light, connect with them by breathing through your heart to harmonize your body's rhythms between your heart and mind. You may want to have a journal by your side or a tape player to assist you in recalling this high-frequency information.

Many times when we do dimensional travel we will fall asleep in the altered state of consciousness until our mind gets used to being able to hold onto two different worlds at once. When you feel relaxed and balanced within yourself, then rise above to your Higher Self. Ask your Higher Self to guide you to the specific dimension of consciousness that you're from.

You may feel like you just entered into a worm hole. A worm hole is a phenomenon in space that acts as a portal from one world to another. We are able to go through a worm hole with our consciousness instead of a space ship. In fact, our consciousness is the vehicle in which our light body travels both while we are in this human form and not.

Ask to meet the Planetary Beings. They may guide you to a temple or room filled with light or crystals. You may be surrounded in a beautifully colored nature scene. Notice if one particular guide or several are there to greet you. Ask them to show you your Soul Blueprint. Do they have any guidance or wisdom for you at this time? Do they give you any gifts? Do they have healing temples, libraries, or learning centers that you can go into? Just enjoy yourself and remember you can go back any time you'd like to be with your Tribe of Light.

THE STAR TRIBES OF LIGHT

The Star Beings communicate primarily through the light body, which flows through the nervous system and emotional body. The Star Beings have a highly developed intuition through the third eye and through sensitivity in the auric field around the body. The aura senses the environmental energies around you including thought forms, projections, emotional reactions, environmental stimulation and toxicity. Our light body governs the electrical body, which affects the crystalline structure in the brain, the beating of the heart, the meridian system, and the nervous system. This covers a lot of ground in the experience of our body. Star Beings are highly experiential in their approach to life. They learn through experiences and experiments with their life force energy. To them life is contextual. Contact with them physically assists them in grounding and lends emotional safety.

The Star Beings come from the star systems versus planetary systems. Stars by their very nature radiate light from the future.

On the inner levels, Star Beings look like flashes of light around you and out the corner of your eye or a cluster of lights that can be seen as an array of colors. They usually travel in clusters or tribes.

Star Beings bring us the gift of technological advancement, Earth sciences, and healing techniques with light and particularly with sound. Similarities exist between the gifts of the Planetary Beings and the Star Beings, but their expressions are quite distinct. The Planetary Beings are methodical, grounded, peaceful, and mentally superior; the Star Beings are childlike, quick thinking, genius-oriented, and emotionally sensitive.

Gift of Inner Genius

If one word could capture the essence of the Star Beings it would be "brilliant." They have the gift of inner genius in them. Souls that reflect this divine heritage are highly creative and playful, adventurous, curious, musically oriented, and whizzes on the computer. They do great with light, color, and sound healing, and are the true indigo children of our time. With their high levels of energy, they think so fast, they don't stay on one topic of conversation for long.

This gives them the advantage of being able to talk about ten different things at once. Truly multidimensional, they can experience many things at one time. When they get focused on something, you can't get their attention even for a minute. They are able to see outside the box of the old world structures because they are the visionaries and inventors of the future. The Star Beings are constantly being flooded with ah-ha ideas as if they're tapped into the "universal field of all possibilities."

The Star Beings have a tendency to travel a lot, their needs somehow magically being met along the way. That's because Star Beings have more crystals than other beings in their brain structure. These crystals radiate out thought forms and emotions that magnetize energy around them for manifestation. However, due to their highly developed nervous system—with their emotional sensitivity and mental telepathy being so advanced—they can easily get overwhelmed by environmental toxins, chemicals in foods (particularly ones that affect the neuro-transmitters in the brain like MSG, artificial flavorings, and food colorings), other people's negative emotions and thought forms, and high surges of energy such as electrical power poles. Their sensitivity, when ungrounded through the heart, can cause them to show ADD/ADHD symptoms.

Elements of Nature

When scientists studied the structural elements of the physical body, they found that we're comprised of the same elements found in star dust. Perhaps we are all little bursts of "star light, star bright" in the making. There is actually what's called star nurseries, for example, where stars are being created in the Eagle Nebula. Wouldn't it be awesome to see the birth of a star!

When light from the stars enters the Earth, it grounds itself through the elements of nature such as trees, rock formations, and crystalline structures within the Earth. Therefore, nature can be extremely helpful to re-balance and ground souls that come from this lineage. When clusters of Star Beings incarnate into physical form, they enter into indigenous tribes to integrate and ground their presence on Earth. The Dolphins and Aboriginals are excellent examples of tribes of Star Beings that are still intact.

As they begin their journey, they keep this connection and understanding of the Earth's rhythms. They will apply this ability to Earth sciences as a group consciousness in the future.

When a soul that comes from this lineage is in balance, their seventh crown chakra is wide open as they interpret the language of light through their sixth "third eye" chakra, which then would channel into their heart chakra. Most Star Beings maintain the seventh chakra open, allowing in tremendous amounts of light, into the pineal gland at the top of the head. This acts as a conduit for spirit.

That light needs to flow uninterrupted into the heart chakra. If it doesn't, it will cause an energy jam in the medulla oblongata at the base of the brain, which gives these souls ADD/ADHD behavior symptoms. Beyond these symptoms, the Star Beings have genius potential that begs to be discovered and brought out.

The heart can shut down by being empathetic to chaotic emotions and negative thought forms from the people and environment around them, then resisting the energy created. This resistance is the fear of being overwhelmed by a sea of energy they've forgotten how to manage. You can't lie to these Star Being souls.

Their level of intuition is unparalleled. They require the safety of unconditional love, and can feel your subconscious fears and judgments even if they're not said aloud or directed at them personally. They hear and feel these emotions and judgments energetically. And if they're not strong in their divine connection, this will bring out their inadequacies and fears of being unlovable.

It can appear that the Star Beings, with their childlike nature, are attention-oriented. This is because they live so much in the moment that they sense it when the people around them are not present. They start reacting to that person to get them back into the present. People often confuse love and attention to mean the same thing, but it is not.

Attention is conditional love based on the personality or ego; Divine Love is the All That Is—it is all encompassing and exists only in the present moment. Divine Love accesses the field of all possibilities, which the Star Beings are masters of.

As emotional geniuses, they are extremely gifted at identifying emotional reactions, which can give them insight into what's going to happen next. They can read the energy matrix of the collective unconscious, which allows them to patent and predict future trends if they desire to use their creativity for that purpose.

Examples of modern-day souls who relate to the Star Being Tribe of Light are:

- Mozart
- Bradley Cooper
- Emma Stone
- Leonardo di Caprio
- Marianne Williamson
- David Bowie
- Taylor Swift

- Anderson Cooper
- Amanda Gorman
- Bruce Lee
- Ashton Kutcher
- Mila Kunis
- Cameron Diaz
- Jack Black

The Pleiades from the star system known as the seven sisters or the kite is one of the closest Star colonies to us. This particular colony trains Beings of Light in the laws of Earth physics to prepare them to come into human form in the physical dimension. Star families can come from star systems much farther away to make their contribution to Earth and the family of humanity. Just like the Planetary Beings, they come in through the gateway of Orion and can go into a training period with the Pleiades. Other examples of Star tribes are the Dolphins, Mayans, Celtics, and Greeks, gypsies, indigo children and Lemurians.

Meditation

Now that you have cleared and re-centered your emotional body by breathing through your heart center, call forth to the electric blue soul star in the eighth chakra above your head to begin streaming from it a blue liquid light to balance your electrical system and nervous system. This light is like a vitamin to your electrical body.

As this liquid blue light is streaming through you, allow it to overflow into each chakra— starting at the head—to open, balance, and align your seventh chakra, overflowing into the sixth chakra in the brow of the forehead to open, balance, and align, overflowing into the fifth chakra in the throat to open, balance, and align, overflowing into the fourth chakra in the heart center to open, balance, and align, overflowing into the third chakra in the solar plexus to open, balance and align, overflowing into the second chakra in the navel to open, balance and align, and overflowing into the first chakra in the perineum at the base of the body to open, balance and align. Take your time with each. Then allow the liquid blue light to connect to a golden disc of light about a foot below your feet. This harmonizes you with the Earth's electrical energy field to help you ground your energy.

From this space, ask the Star Beings from this Tribe of Light to come forth and enfold you. Notice what color of light comes toward you, and how the Beings feel. Ask them to take you back to the specific star system you're from and inquire about your purpose on Earth. Ask them to place you in a star or a dolphin chamber of light to be rejuvenated and taught what you need to know while you sleep or meditate.

GALACTIC, PLANETARY, STAR SYSTEM GUIDE

The celestial bodies have been a fascination to humankind throughout time. We gaze upon them, create rituals, ceremonies, and plant crops around their cycles. The celestial realms constantly radiate and broadcast messages and essence feelings that represent the sentient beings that dwell upon them in the form of light rays. But this communication is not one-sided though.

We also send our messages and essence feelings to them as well. The distance isn't nearly the factor we might think it is. Through our intention of conscious communication, messages can be relayed instantly.

The positive effects of developing a relationship with these Beings include profound shifts in consciousness, new life perspectives, and enhanced mental and intuitive abilities. If you feel like you come from a Star, Planetary, or Galactic Tribe of Light and want to know what heritage you resonate with, use a pendulum or muscle testing to practice with the list below.

See if one is revealed to you as you go into meditation and ask your Tribe of Light to take you to the system you're from.

Keep in mind some of the names and numbered systems are not the true name of a star system, but rather its location. By being in contact with your Tribe of Light, you may discover its original name. Each system represents a quality essence and consciousness in which that system governs. (M1- M108 represent: clusters, globular clusters, constellations, galaxies, and nebulas. Some examples of ones that have been numbered are listed below; many have not been named other than by category.)

Planets, stars, moons, suns, and galaxy systems:

A	Algol	Alnilam
Acamar	Alhena	Alnitak
Achernar	Alioth	Alphard
Adhara	Alkaid	Alphecca
Albireo	Almach	Alpheratz
Alcor	Alnair	Alrisha
Alcyone	Alnilam	Altair
Aldebaran	Alnitak	Andromeda Galaxy
Alderamin	Alpha Centauri	Antares
Algenib	Alludra	Aquarius
Algieba	Al Nasl	Aquila

Arcturus	Carina	Diphda
Aries	Cassiopeia	Draco
Arneb	Castor	Dschubba
Auriga	Centaurus	Dubhe
Ascella	Cepheus	E
Asellus Australis	Cetus	Electra (Pleiades)
Asellus Borealis	Cheleb	Elnath
B	Chiron	Eltanin
Bellatrix	Coma Berenices	El Tarf
Beta Corvii	Cor Caroli	Enif
Betelgeuse	Corona Borealis	Epsilon Leonis
Big Dipper	Corvus	Epsilon Perseii
Bootes	Cygnus	Equuleus
C	Cursa	Eridanus
Camelopardalis	D	F
Cancer	Delphinus	Fomalhaut
Canus Venatici	Dabih	G
Canis Major	Delta Cephei	Gamma persei
Canis Minor	Delta Cygni	Gamma Piscium
Canopus	Delta Ophiuchi	Gemini
Capella	Deneb	Gertab
Caph	Deneb Algedi	Giedi
Capricornus	Denebola	Gienah

Gomeisa	Kaus Borealis	M57 (Ring Nebula)
Graffias	Kochab	M97 (Owl Nebula)
H	Kornephoros	M104 (Sombrero Galaxy)
Hadar	L	Markab
Hale-Bopp	Lacerta	Mars
Hamal	Leo	Matar
Han	Libra	Media
H & Chi Persei	Little Dipper	Megrez
Helios (the Sun)	Lupus	Menkalinan
Helix Nebula	Lyra	Menkar
Hercules	Lesath	Menkent
Hipparchus	Luna (the Moon)	Merak
Horsehead Nebula	M	Milky Way Galaxy
Hyades Cluster	M1 (Crab Nebula)	Mintaka
Hydra	M3 (Globular Cluster)	Mercury
I	M8 (Lagoon Nebula)	Merope (Pleiades)
Iota Aurigae	M13 (Hercules Cluster)	Mesarthim
Iota Orionis	M16 (Eagle Nebula)	Microscopium
Izar	M20 (Trifid Nebula)	Mintaka
J	M27 (Dumbell Nebulla)	Mira
Jupiter	M33 (Pinwheel Galaxy)	Mirach
K	M42 (Orion Nebula)	Mirfak
Kaus Australis	M51 (Whirl Pool Galaxy)	Mirzam

Muphrid	Pleiades	Sagittarius
Mizar	Pluto	Saiph
Monoceros	Polaris	Sargas
N	Pollux	Saturn
Nashira	Porrima	Saturn Nebula
Neptune	Praisepe	Scat
North American Nebula	Procyon	Scheat
Nunki	Puppus	Schedar
O	Pyxis	Scorpius
Omega Centauri	R	Sculptor
Ophiuchus	Rasalgethi	Scutum
Orion	Rasalhague	Serpens
Orion Nebula	Rastaban	Sextans
P	Regulus	Shaula
Parsec	Rigel	Shaula
Pegasus	Rosette Nebula	Sheratin
Perseus	Ruchbah	Sigma Scorpii
Petra	S	Sirius
Phact	Sabik	Spica
Phecda	Sadalmelik	Swan Nebula
Pi Sagittarii	Sadalsud	T
Pisces	Sadr	Tarazed
Piscis Austrinus	Sagitta	Taurus

Tau Scorpii	Zubenelgenubi
Theta aurigae	Zubeneschamali
Thuban	Great Central Sun.
Triangulum Galaxy	
Tsih	
U	
Unuk	
Uranus	
V	
Vega	
Veil Nebula	
Venus	
Vindemiatrix	
Virgo	
Vulpecula	
W	
Wei	
Z	
Zeta Cygni	
Zeta Perseii	
Zeta Tauri	
Zosma	

ANGELIC TRIBE OF LIGHT

Angels are miraculous Beings of Light who act as "living resources" in our daily lives. They are the messengers of the Divine enfolding us in quality essences such as love, joy, faith, strength, courage, etc... Quality essences are the nectar that feeds the human soul, giving us the strength of character to fulfill our Divine Destiny. Angels offer us this gift by sending forth rays of light from the essence of their Being that enfolds our soul. Angelic Beings are in service to the Flames of Creation.

The Flames of Creation are held sacred within the Temples of Light governed by the Elohim Angels. In these temples, they absorb the quality essence, inspirations, and rays of light to bring forth and enfold a human soul. This may be a creative idea, a work of art, a good deed, a noble cause, even compassion or understanding. Infinite sources of Angels are in creation because God is an infinite creator. For every creation and prayer spoken, there are Angels to enfold and bless them.

Angelic Beings are not only in service to the family of humanity, but also to many other causes of Spirit, such as the Ascended Masters or the Nature Kingdom. They can cross connect to any other Tribes of Light in support of the higher causes they desire to be in service to.

One important activity that reflects this is within the Nature Kingdom. For example, Archangel Ariel governs a group of Angelic nature spirits called Devas. The Cosmic Christ Angels are in service to the Creative Flame of the Ascended Master Jesus. There is Mother Mary and the Sacred Heart Angels, and Kwan Yin and the Angels of Mercy. Each of the Ascended Host governs a tribe of Angels in service to their higher cause.

Churches and hospitals also attract concentrations of different Angelic Hosts to support the prayers being said. This is why people instantly feel better when they walk into churches, temples, monasteries, nunneries, Native American ritual sites and other sacred places; these environments have been qualified to a higher frequency of spirit. The Living Host of Angels gathered there to serve those who are praying. They can be instantly felt as a calming, healing presence. *Higher Conversations* is the third book in this series, and highlights more information about communicating with these special beings.

Angelic Beings are service-oriented in direct relation with the family of humanity. The basic foundation to any Angelic Being is service through Divine Love. They carry the Divine Love ray first and foremost, whether through a service rendered, a prayer, or a blessing. They care deeply about others empathetically. As they feel what others are feeling, they're sympathetic to them in a counseling way. With this gift, they take on others' feelings and re-harmonize them to a more peaceful, loving state. This gift makes them excellent counselors, nurses, caregivers, and healers. Angelic Beings thrive on living simple lifestyles. They always strive to bring harmony and peace into the relationships of their lives, whether it is in partnership, family, friendships, work relations, or even with people they don't know.

Angelic Beings communicate through their heart center, which relates to the deeper feelings within a person versus strictly emotional reactions. Those who come from this lineage have the gift of listening and speaking the language of the soul, which govern the heart's wisdom. They use this gift to enfold those they're comforting with the essence of love, peace, patience, forgiveness, faith, hope, and healing.

Their depth of intuition is from their soul's wisdom. The soul's wisdom is also known as the heart's wisdom. With each emotion is a deeper feeling, and with each feeling is a wisdom gained in your soul's evolutions. The more often you can return back to and ground yourself in your soul's wisdom, the more graceful and compassionate life flows in a synchronicity of miracles, harmonious perfection and divine alignment. The soul's wisdom and Angelic consciousness communicate through the sacred heart of an individual, thus expanding unconditional and divine love in the world as a gift from the Divine.

Angelic Beings innately have developed within them the gift of unconditional love. Through the power of unconditional love, they serve as heart healers to those with a troubled heart. Angelic Beings are particularly interested in being of service to people in need around them—their family members, friends, and communities.

Angelic Beings are the ultimate humanitarians, always sensitive to their relationships and the feelings of others. Their sense of unconditional love and nurturance offers an incredible comfort. Others love to bask in the warm glow of that love. Angelic Beings are often gifted at praying for and blessing others—activities of Spirit that act as the conduit for creation, manifestation, healing, and insight.

Most Angelic Beings don't yet realize what a gold mine they have in their ability to communicate directly with the Heart of Creation, God, Source, and the Angels through this spiritual art. Angelic Beings usually seem more passive in nature, but the gift of prayer and blessing is a powerhouse of resources, the cornerstone of manifestation and co-creation. They simply need to remember to use it. If you have a friend that is of t he Angelic Tribe of Light, ask them to pray for you and watch the synchronicity of miracles that will come from it.

Angelic Beings are empathic healers and prayer practitioners bringing forth the blessings of Grace more than action-oriented doers. Even though Angelic Beings fundamentally prefer harmony and peace, if their childhoods were chaotic, then their nervous system patterns may constantly attract chaos into their lives.

Because they are service-oriented beings by their nature, they can become addicted to trying to heal, help, fix, and save people. They experience anything but simplicity and peace for themselves. Being so highly empathic to the needs of others can work against them if they don't understand how to balance their empathic awareness. If they are not connected within themselves to the source of their Divine Love, they may not know how to discern their own feelings and needs from others. This can cause them to over-care for others, overwhelm themselves, and engage in their own survival issues.

The key to empathizing is not to resist the feeling, but *allow* yourself to feel. Resisting the feeling will cause your heart to shut down and render you helpless and overwhelmed. Instead breathe into your heart in long rhythmic breaths. Become one with the feeling. Through the power of your breath, you'll begin to transform the energy you feel into conscious awareness through your heart's wisdom. Your soul or Angels can guide you toward taking the action which will be in the highest good of all. The action to transform a situation usually begins with a prayer or blessing instead of a physical change.

Do Not Underestimate the Power of Your Prayers and Blessings to Transform a Situation Back to Harmonious Perfection.

Prayers and blessings are the "living instruments" for Angelic Beings acting as tools of Pure Love and Light. Once you have re-harmonized your own energy field by breathing through your heart, and have prayed for or blessed the situation, wait to be guided on any action to take at that point. When you do, harmony, peace, and simplicity will instantly return to your life.

One of the most well-known angels is Archangel Michael, who acts as a protector and warrior Angel to those in need. The seven Archangels are particularly well known in the Catholic and Jewish

Traditions: Michael, Chamuel, Jophiel, Gabriel, Uriel, Raphael, Zadkiel.

Angels are referred to in almost all of the major religions and scriptures. They have been depicted in beautiful works of art and music throughout history. They have inspired a myriad of stories from people who could feel or see them in moments of their life. Angels sit much closer to us than we realize.

Many different legions of Angelic Tribes exist in which you may be of service to. Each tribe represents a quality essence that reflects the service they render. Below is a list of different Angelic Tribes to pray with. Use a pendulum or muscle testing to locate *your* Angelic Family of Light. Keep in mind that souls in this divine heritage have often worked with different legions. They develop additional quality essences to be of service to the family of humanity within their souls' evolution.

Examples of souls who are related to the Angelic Tribe of Light are:

- Fred Roger's from Mr. Rogers Neighborhood
- Mother Teresa
- Malala Yousafzai
- Reese Witherspoon
- Sarah McLachlan
- Christopher Reeve
- Drew Barrymore
- Whitney Houston
- Denzel Washington
- Kate Winslet

Meditation

If you feel like you resonate to this Family of Light, a great way to connect with them is to center yourself within the heart's wisdom of your soul. Breathe deeply into your heart center, and allow yourself to begin to expand your heart center by remembering a loving thought, memory, or vision. This process begins to train your heart to the frequency of unconditional love and compassion.

Now that you have opened to the sacred space of your heart's wisdom, shift your awareness to your soul. Ask your soul to connect a stream of light from the jewel in its heart center into the jewel of light in your heart center. Notice how it feels as you begin to expand into the light of your soul's magnificence, feeling the depth of love you have to all living things, how we're all connected, how beautiful all of life is. By expanding your consciousness into this much love, it is easy to feel your connection to your Angelic Family of Light and the gifts they have to share with you.

Now, call to your Angelic Tribe of Light and watch as the beautiful Angelic Beings come swirling in around you in all their grace and love, enfolding you in the warmth of their light, peace, and love. Ask your Angelic Tribe of Light to show you the gift of your service to others. Ask how they can assist you.

From your heart, convey the prayers of its wisdom to your Angelic Family of Light, either for yourself, others, or the world, so they can bless them with their love for a synchronicity of miracles to unfold. Notice their joy to be of service to your heart's desires. Ask them to take you into the Temples of Light and the sacred healing chambers to help you heal issues in your life or to pass through you to bring forth healing energy to another soul.

Angel Healings

Ask your Angelic Tribe of Light to enfold you in an Angel Healing while you sleep or meditate. Angel Healings are a wonderful way to clear any discord out of your emotional body. You may want to place your right hand on your third eye or crown chakra and your left hand just below your navel or on your heart.

This will assist in balancing your head and heart energies. These Angels will channel directly through your heart center into the space around you and begin to clear your aura, balance your chakras, and re-harmonize your emotional body back to a place of peace. They usually take ten to twenty minutes to complete their work. These are great to do on children, pets, partners, and people who need healing.

Gathering within your heart all your love, adoration, and gratitude, send this forth to the presence of your soul and Angelic Tribe of Light for the service they have rendered to you. The more love you send to them, the more love they send back to you. This ignites an abundance of unconditional love to radiate within you and the world around you. You'll be a walking blessing of peace and love to all.

ANGELIC GUIDE

There are 144 thousand ascended master, Archangels and Elohim Angels who govern the Rays of Creation that make up part of the Spiritual Hierarchy.

Archangels

Aishim	Elyon	Mihr	Shekinah
Akatriel	En Suf	Nathaniel	Shushienae
Amarushaya	Fortunata	Nisroc	Sizouse
Amitiel	Gabriel	Ongkanaon	Soqed Hozi
Anachel	Galgaliel	Ooniemme	Sstiel
Anael	Gethsemane	Oromasis	Stamera

Ariel	Hadraniel	Paschar	Tabris
Astrea	Hamied	Phanuel	Tahariel
Aurora	Iofiel	Propator	Tophiel
Baruch	Isphan Darmaz	Ramaela	Uriel
Boel	Israfel	Raphael	Uzziel
Cassiel	Jamaerah	Raziel	Vretil
Cerviel	Jeu	Remiel	Zacharael
Chamuel	Jophiel	Remliel	Zacharael
Charis	Kaeylarae	Rikbiel	Zadkiel
Charmiene	Metatron	Sabriel	Zagzagel
Chayyiel	Micah	Sandalphon	Zaphkiel
Dominion	Michael	Shamsheil	Zophiel

Angelic Tribes

ANGELIC TRIBES OF THE RAYS OF CREATION:	
Angels of Divine Creation	Angels of Divine Order
Angels of Divine Harmony	Angels of Divine Peace
Angels of Divine Illumination	Angels of Divine Perfection
Angels of Divine Love	Angels of Divine Power
Angels of Divine Manifestation	Angels of Divine Purity
Angels of Divine Mastery	Angels of Divine Vision
Angels of Divine Oneness	Angels of Divine Wisdom

ANGELIC TRIBES OF THE TREE OF LIFE:	
Aralim	Cherubim
Ashim	Detritii
Auphanim	Detritii
Beni Elohim	Elohim
Chaioth ha Qadesh	Melachim
Chasmalim	Seraphim

OTHER ANGELS:	
Adoration Angels	Cosmic Christ Angels
Angels of Freedom	Creation Angels
Angels of Grace	Earth Angels
Angels of Healing	Fire Angels
Angels of High Magic	Golden Light Angels
Angels of Justice	Golden Miracle Angels
Angels of Liberty	Gratitude Angels
Angels of Light	Great Central Sun Angels
Angels of Mercy	Great Cosmic Angels
Angels of Sacred Fire	Listening Angels
Angels of the Rose Temple	Music Angels
Angels of Victory	The Essential Angels
Ascension Angels	Unknown Angels
Blue Lightning Sword Angels	Violet Flame Angels
Christmas Angels	

ELOHIM ANGELS, CREATION ANGELS, & COSMIC ANGELS	
Adonai Ha-Aretz	Jehovah
Adonai Malakh	Jehovah Eloah Vadaath
Cosmic Angels	Jehovah Elohim
Eheieh	Jehovah Tsabaoth
El	Shaddai El Chai
Eloah Vadaath	The Holy Spirit
Elohim Gibor	The Silent Watcher
Elohim Tzabaoth	

ASCENDED MASTERS
TRIBE OF LIGHT

Ascended Masters are considered a Tribe of Light, but like the Nature Kingdom, their origin will be found in the Cosmic, Galactic, Planetary, Star, or Angelic Tribes of Light. So even though you may align with the Ascended Master Tribe of Light, they may be considered a secondary Tribe of Light in which you have worked with the living and Ascended Masters in past, present, or future lives. They have tremendous value and power in being able to teach us about our divine heritage, the right use of universal law, and our soul gifts. Like the Nature Kingdom they compliment our soul's journey in physical form.

The Ascended Master Tribe of Light represents the potential within each of us to be a living master. An Ascended Master is a soul like you and me that has walked this Earth in human form and became masters of the universal laws of creation in which we are all bound to. This took tremendous focus, discipline, and love over lifetimes to accomplish.

Each lifetime of conscious service would raise their vibration and increase their life force energy to be able to deliver the gift of love. They came here to fulfill their Divine Plans, which each of us have a commitment to fulfill before we can move forward into our next expression of divine love. Once their destiny was fulfilled they can ascend to a higher consciousness of service into a dimensional world above the physical realm.

Ascension happens when a soul has raised its consciousness to a level of awareness in which it is no longer bound to the karmic wheel of life and death. A soul can then freely choose to ascend into its next evolution. What makes this so spectacular is that these beings have brought so much light into the cells of their body that they do not experience a physical death. Rather, they ascend and take their physical form with them. Their physical form becomes perfected as it rises into the higher octaves.

Ascended Masters live in an octave of light above us, known as etheric retreats. The etheric retreats of the masters are Temples of Light where the Ascended Masters teach to students of the light, often referred to as "Chelas." Students of the universal laws and higher truths can travel to these retreats on the inner levels in an etheric garment of light.

The etheric garment of light is your etheric double or Light Body. Most often you travel in your Light Body when you are asleep or in meditation. It is a form of dimensional travel, referred to in the earlier chapters on the dimensional bodies. Held within the etheric retreats are halls of the akashic and etheric records and great libraries of the histories of the family of humanity and higher teachings of universal principles. There are also other consciousness tools such as a mirror that reveals to you all your past lives and experiences and an atomic accelerator that assists a soul in speeding up the atoms of its physical being for healing, ascension, or raising consciousness.

The retreats are also gathering places of great light on the planet where the Ascended Host will come together and focus its light, love, and wisdom to the Earth and the family of humanity. These retreats are often located on vortexes or ley lines within the Earth's electronic energy grid. They can be located like small cities of lights within mountain ranges, in caves, in caverns on the ocean floor, or above deserts.

Each retreat represents a different energy or universal principle that is to be brought forth into this world and has members of the Ascended Host who govern the energy of that specialized energy ray. The Ascended Masters have been known to live within different cultures of people such as the temples within the Amazon and Peru, with the Mayans in Chitzen Itza, the monasteries within the Himalayas, the Temple of Luxor in Egypt, Atlantis, Lemuria, and the Jade Temple in China. Many accounts of the influence of the Ascended Masters and their teachings have been passed down to us.

The most common story of ascension is that of Jesus in the cave after being on the cross when he went through the resurrection. Ascension can exist in many forms. There is the kind in which your physical body rises above the ground. This classic form requires an immense amount of inner light to pull off. Then there is the resurrection form, in which you die and come back, raising your physical body into light within several days to a week from the time of death.

Then there is the kind I believe to be easiest and most popular—consciously dying. This is when you feel complete with your experience on Earth and have permission from your soul to go on to your next life. Your consciousness guides the light of your soul above your physical body, leaving it behind. You move forward in your etheric body, but you are still not bound to the karmic wheel. This allows you to not become sick or have an accident in order to transition; it's your conscious choice.

Essentially, to consciously ascend, you would enter into a deep state of inner peace, allowing yourself to connect with your Divine Source and will yourself to rise above your body and merge with the higher worlds. You do this when you meditate or sleep naturally; the only difference is that you are allowing your consciousness to remain connected to your physical body unlike when you sleep or meditate.

When you consciously transition, you will your consciousness to *disconnect* from your body. If you plan on consciously ascending when your time has come, it's a good idea to know where you're being guided to go next. If you don't know, make sure you have turned over your life force to your I Am Presence or God Self to guide you appropriately. Otherwise, you might find yourself wandering around aimlessly as a discarnate ghost.

When any of us die, we exit with the use of our etheric body. The difference is that when through ascension in one of these three forms, you're not bound to have to come back to the karmic wheel of life and death. You can be free of the karmic wheel when your soul has learned all it needed to learn to unconditionally give the gift of love that you originally agreed to bring forth as a steward of the Light of God, and fulfill your Soul Blueprint.

The *Tibetan Book of the Dead* teaches that when you're living your life so completely each day with no regrets or unfinished business or distractions from your love for God—living in the present moment with all of life—you are whole. In this wholeness, you are complete. Most people die with unresolved conflicts within them and must come back to resolve them. In the process, they shift their karma to dharma, a life of service learned from your life lessons. Instead of doing this unconsciously, they can act in conscious ways of compassionate action.

Souls that resonate to this Tribe of Light have often lived past lives living in monasteries, holy temples, mystery schools, and sacred power spots. There, they have been taught the right use of universal laws and divine wisdom for co-creation. These souls are devoted to the path of the heart through compassion, and experience balance between the heart's wisdom and the Higher Self's wisdom.

This gives them the ability to walk between the worlds of heaven and Earth as a living master with a strong mind of determination and a strong heart of compassion. These souls have an immense amount of inner strength and character and are very stable, dependable, and noble. They have an instinct to protect those less fortunate.

However, these souls are not caretakers like the Angelic souls. They protect others from harm or unfair circumstances out of the nobility in their hearts to do the right thing, but it ends there. They would prefer to teach you how to fish, rather than fish for you. This makes them excellent teachers. They have been devoted students and know what it takes to evolve the character of a soul.

They tend to be loners, because they've lived the majority of their lifetimes in solitude focused on their studies of a higher truth. And even though they will love and protect their families, they still like their alone time to be with Spirit. They do this through meditating, tai chi, yoga, fishing, golfing, woodworking, hiking in nature, or some other activity.

These beings would rather be leaders than followers. They do not like emotional distractions to the purpose they are dedicated to. The Ascended Master Tribe of Light practices the art of mastery over their emotions, thoughts, actions, and spoken words. They practice the activities of their Higher Presence, not their personalities. They are known for their services of "compassionate action"; they have taken-action to make the world a better place by bringing a situation back into divine alignment.

The Ascended Masters are sometimes referred to as the Great White Brotherhood. The word "White" is in reference to the White Light of God. As a color, white frequency absorbs all other color frequencies that help dispense all the rays of co-creation.

The word "Brotherhood" implies unity of all humanity and the Ascended Host working in cooperation with one another. The term is not intended to exclude the feminine presence. Rather, the Ascended Masters are not focused on the human personality expressions of male/ female, right/wrong, good/bad, rich/poor, white/black/ yellow/red, but rather the universal truth that we are all one and come from one source.

There are many different orders of Ascended Masters dedicated to different God attributes. Attributes are positive character traits that we as humans develop in the wisdom of our understanding and mastery. Ascended Masters teach these attributes through the law of life experiences.

Quality essences are feelings that strengthen the soul, which the Archangels teach. God attributes have been taught for centuries in monasteries, temples, and mystery schools to develop the character needed to fulfill a higher service in this world. These attributes can look like virtue, patience, honesty, loyalty, strength, and more. They often relate to a quality essence or feeling to support it. For instance, the attribute of having strength of character is often supported by the quality essence of courage.

When Ascended Masters have completed the service they desired to fulfill on behalf of their Soul Blueprint, they will evolve to their next level of service. As in any hierarchy, when one is complete with the cycle of their service, they move on to the next evolutionary spiral and open a space for the next soul to uphold the Flame of Light. The cycles in the spiritual hierarchy vary, but most have a two thousand year span. The cycles they follow align with astrological and solar evolutions.

For instance, we are currently in a shifting of the Spiritual Hierarchy from the family of humanity living within the dispensation of light in the Piscean Age (with Jesus being a Master Teacher) and are moving into the Aquarian Age (in which St.

Germain brings forth the teachings of the Violet Transmuting Flame of Manifestation and Freedom).

We can also see these shifts in the Tree of Life as root races evolve within the family of humanity. We are currently the fifth root race of Earth and are in the fifth cycle of consciousness moving toward the sixth cycle.

When the root race completes its seven cycles of evolution, the soul group moves to its next evolutionary path and another soul group comes forth. Earth provides a training ground for conscious evolution and co-creation.

Some members of the Ascended Hosts were in previous root races before us. They now assist us in our evolution, as we will assist the root races that come after us. Lemurians were a root race, and Atlanteans were another root race. At the height of both civilizations, Earth changes happened that released them from Earth to their next expression.

Similarly, the planet makes room for the next root race to come forward. For instance, the Mayans, Incans, and Anasazi Indians disappeared as the Aboriginals are disappearing now. These indigenous people are perhaps another root race of consciousness that is leaving or has already left.

Soul groups travel together in their conscious evolution. Each group of souls continues connecting lifetime after lifetime to learn new perspectives. Ultimately, they gain the soul's wisdom needed to fulfill their Soul Blueprint. As part of the soul group, sometimes you play a child, sometimes a parent. Sometimes you are a warrior, sometimes you are a slave. Sometimes you are rich, sometimes you are poor.

The soul gains an immense amount of wisdom from all these situations so they can have greater understanding in their service to another soul. Keep in mind that the soul is the dimensional aspect of self that is having these karmic action/reaction experiences so it can transcend into the compassionate action of its dharma. That means in each lifetime, you gain a thread of wisdom to add to the tapestry of your Divine Plan.

When the root race completes its seven cycles of evolution, the soul group moves to its next evolutionary path and another soul group comes forth. Earth provides a training ground for conscious evolution and co-creation.

Some members of the Ascended Hosts were in previous root races before us. They now assist us in our evolution, as we will assist the root races that come after us. Lemurians were a root race, and Atlanteans were another root race. At the height of both civilizations, Earth changes happened that released them from Earth to their next expression. Similarly, the planet makes room for the next root race to come forward. For instance, the Mayans, Incans, and Anasazi Indians disappeared as the Aboriginals are disappearing now. These indigenous people are perhaps another root race of consciousness that is leaving or has already left.

Soul groups travel together in their conscious evolution. Each group of souls continues connecting lifetime after lifetime to learn new perspectives. Ultimately, they gain the soul's wisdom needed to fulfill their Soul Blueprint. As part of the soul group, sometimes you play a child, sometimes a parent. Sometimes you are a warrior, sometimes you are a slave. Sometimes you are rich, sometimes you are poor.

The soul gains an immense amount of wisdom from all these situations so they can have greater understanding in their service to another soul. Keep in mind that the soul is the dimensional aspect of self that is having these karmic action/reaction experiences so it can transcend into the compassionate action of its dharma. That means in each lifetime, you gain a thread of wisdom to add to the tapestry of your Divine Plan.

These souls are destiny oriented; meaning everything they do has a purpose. They feel a strong need to make a difference in the world and improve the quality of life for all who genuinely seek the higher path. They love a good challenge that requires discipline, will, devotion, and mastery of their inner authority.

Those who resonate with the Ascended Master Tribe of Light make great leaders in their communities and can be good authority figures for those searching for a mentor to guide them in the higher values of life. They tend to have good boundaries with others because they have a high code of ethics in which honor, loyalty, honesty, strength, and courage are priorities.

Examples of Modern-day souls who are related to the Ascended Master Tribe of Light are:

- Padre Pio
- Carolyn Myss
- Lao Tzu
- Edgar Cayce

- Paulo Coelho
- Ram Dass
- Joel Osteen
- Gary Zukav
- Wayne Dyer
- Byron Katie
- Dr. Joe Dispenza

Meditation

Doing this meditation for 15 minutes at night before retiring and in the morning before beginning your day will work wonders. If you resonate to this Tribe of Light, a great way to connect with the beings in the family is by doing the *Masters Meditation*.

First, call forth to your Beloved I Am Presence to enfold you in the "Spiraling Blue Flame of the Ascended Master Octave." Then still all outer activity of both mind and body through focusing on your breath flowing in and out of your heart center. Make certain you won't be disturbed. After becoming very still, picture and feel your body enveloped in a dazzling white light. After five minutes of holding this picture, recognize and feel the connection between your outer self and your mighty God Presence within, focusing your attention on the heart center and visualizing it as a golden sun. Allow the brilliant white light and the golden sun to come into a rhythm of harmonious perfection with one another.

Then acknowledge out loud or silently, "I now joyously accept the fullness of the mighty God Presence—the pure Christ Light."

Feel the great brilliancy of the light intensify in every cell of your body for at least ten minutes longer. Then close the meditation with this command: "I Am a child of the light, I love the light, I serve the light, I live in the light, I Am protected, illumined, supplied, sustained, by the light, and I Am blessed by the light."

Now that you have harmonized your inner and outer worlds, call forth the Ascended Master Tribe of Light to guide you to an etheric retreat or Temple of Light that would serve your highest good in the fulfillment of your Soul Blueprint.

ASCENDED MASTER GUIDE

Angels who govern the Rays of Creation that make up part of the Spiritual Hierarchy.

Astrea	Goddess of Justice, and Goddess of Victory
Babaji	Goddess of Liberty
Casimir Poseidon	Goddess of Light
Chananda	Goddess of Love
Cuzco	Hilarion
David Lloyd	Himalaya
Djwal khul	Jesus
El Morya	Kali
Enoch	Krishna
Eriel	Kwan Yin
Goddess of Freedom	Lady Leto

Lady Nada	Pallas Athena
Lady Portia	Paul the Venetian
Lanello	Pelleur
Lord Ganesha	Serpis Bey
Lord Guatama Buddha	St. Germain
Lord Kuthumi	Surya
Lord Lantos	Tabor
Lord Maha Chohan/Great Divine Director	Tara
Lord Maitreya	The Brotherhood and Sisterhood of the Ascended Christ
Lord Shiva	
Lord Vishnu	The Brotherhood of the Golden Robe
Melchezidek	The Brotherhood of the Precipitation
Meru	Vaivasvata Manu
Meta	Zarathustra
Mother Mary	

There are 144 thousand Ascended Master, Archangels and Elohim.

NATURE KINGDOM
TRIBE OF LIGHT

The Nature Kingdom is sustained from two different groups of Beings. One group is within the Angelic Tribe of Light called Devas. The other group is within the Star Tribe of Light called Elementals. These beings volunteered to come forth and sustain the Earth with their essence. They have an immense amount of purity and innocence in their intent of service to the soul of Earth. They focus on the harmony and abundance of the Earth. Through this service, they support the family of humanity in the resources needed to fulfill their needs.

The Nature Kingdom is located in what we call the astral realm. It was intended to be in service to the family of humanity with the resources of the Earth's abundance. The Elementals and Devas are extremely sensitive to the thought forms and emotions of humanity.

They read the electronic imprints of the needs of a person and go forth to fulfill them in the Nature Kingdom. When we do things that imbalance us and our environment, like mining, logging, oil fields, ocean pollution, experimental bombing, animal factories, nuclear waste, over population, waste dumps, air/water/ noise/ light/sound pollution, stripping the Earth of natural resources, and deforestation, these Beings go forth and find ways to transmute and re-harmonize the discord.

They do this mostly through tornadoes, hurricanes, and fires— what we term "natural disasters." Over time, and particularly with the influence of religious dogma and industrialism, a separation between these two Families of Light has existed. Elementals and Devas of the Nature Kingdom have been discounted, overwhelmed, and pushed out of their natural habitats. Our ability to interact with this kingdom has suffered greatly due to humanity's negligence and lack of cooperation.

The Nature Kingdom is filled with an array of delightful, loving beings, who can help us heal and re-balance from our fast-paced lives. It's a magical world filled with faeries, gnomes, Devas, elves, sprites, tree spirits, elementals, crystals, gemstones, animals, dolphins, whales, and many more beings that support the Earth herself and the well-being of the family of humanity.

As we live worlds within worlds in our universal co-existence, the Nature Kingdom sits closest to us, overlapping our physical space. Because we essentially dwell within the same world, it makes communication easier. We simply harmonize to the natural rhythm of the Earth.

We see the Nature Kingdom through the trees, plants, oceans, rivers, animals, stone, and crystals. However, the dimensional world of the Nature Kingdom is seen in etheric forms that dwell in magnificent golden Temples of Light and gardens within the Earth itself, sometimes called Gaia, Hyperborean, or Middle Earth. Most of our mythological characters come from this realm; they were brought into our consciousness by souls that have an inner connection to this world.

The Celtic traditions, Central and Native American Indians, Aboriginals and most all indigenous people are excellent examples of cultures living in co-existence with the Earth and the Nature Kingdom. People in these cultures know how to harmonize with the Earth's rhythms. They communicate with the animal and plant spirits for spiritual guidance and healing. Their whole way of life is filled with ceremonies, rituals, and daily traditions that honor their role as stewards of the Earth.

The Nature Kingdom is of tremendous service to the family of humanity by helping us ground and clear energy, sustain us physically through foods and herbs that heal, as well as supplying us with shelter and the resources that our economies are based on—gold, oil, paper, wood, metal, and more.

We have a tendency to take this Tribe of Light for granted, but without the Nature Kingdom, we couldn't survive. Star Beings and Angels tend to have a special heart connection with the Nature Kingdom, giving them the gift of interspecies communication to the plant and animal kingdom.

Souls connected to this Tribe of Light can communicate with animals and plants, and have an instinctual understanding of healing through herbs and flowers. They are environmentally and emotionally sensitive, are highly creative, and tend to be innocent and childlike. It's hard for these souls to live in a city environment. They would prefer to go barefoot at all times. They tend to be artistic, particularly with natural substances like clay, basket weaving, candle making, nature photography, and woodcarving.

The true stewards of the Earth, these souls have an innate instinct to protect the Nature Kingdom against the greed and ignorance of human commercialism. They are individualistic and like their own space, but work well in communal and village situations, each making a unique contribution to the group.

They have a blend of Angelic and Star Being characteristics, such as healing with nature, herbs, midwifery, veterinarian, farmers, gardeners, they know the rhythms of the Earth through the movement of the stars and the seasons, and through their artistic and musical abilities. They also have a natural instinct for the rhythms of nature and Earth sciences, permaculture, solar energy, and green living.

Archangel Ariel governs over one aspect of the Nature Kingdom called Devas, which are Angelic nature spirits. Devas are beautiful radiant Beings of Light that over-light each species of the plant and animal kingdom. They are the guardians of plants, trees, flowers, animals and all aspects of the Earth itself, using their energetic essence, tending, sustaining, and feeding it through vibration.

There is a Deva for each animal, plant, tree, and flower species, garden, and land masses such as mountain chains, valleys, deserts, forests, rivers, and oceans. When the Devas are working with a land mass or governing a plant species like redwood trees or cabbage plants, they join in a hive-mind as a spirit of that area or species.

A great example is a shaman who can gather information about another area by communicating to a species of nature in his own area. Cities have fewer Devas dwelling in them because less living matter exists there for them to govern.

The Deva sustains these life forms by enfolding them in the quality essences needed to grow and sustain life, just like the Archangels and Cherubs do for human souls, assisting in their evolution. This gives a place on Earth a unique feeling such as a garden that feels peaceful or an area that's a sacred burial site or waters known for healing. This is also why people say that their pets are like Angels, or when animals consciously save a person's life or act as a totem. Sometimes certain plant species represent a healing quality. It's not only the chemical compounds of the plant but the vibrational resonance that heals, as found in flower essences and homeopathic remedies.

A Deva expresses itself energetically through the life form it serves as it supports the needs of that specific life form in its own evolution—as its soul. Without the Deva, the life form would die. If you poison a plant, you poison the Deva within. Devic Beings are receptive to communication of our thoughts and emotions.

The Findhorn Garden, located in Scotland, is one of the best examples of the inner species communication between plants and humans. The classic book *The Secret Life of Plants* is a scientific study of this connection. Bach Flower remedies and Perelandra Flower Essences have bottled the essence of the plant vibration to help balance the subtle energy bodies of our thoughts and emotions.

The Star Beings govern the other aspect of the Nature Kingdom, known as the Elementals. Elementals are the "builders of form." Elementals start out as electronic substances and can grow into a cell, flower, tree, valley, river, planet, solar system, or even galaxy.

Elementals are an aspect of the building blocks of conscious thoughts being directed to them from a conscious life form, such as a Deva, human, Ascended Master, Cosmic Being, or Source. There is also an Elemental Presence that over-lights each human being. It dwells within the aura of a person and becomes an elemental life force energy, which is the accumulation of that person's thoughts and emotions. Its primary role is to materialize "heaven on Earth," focusing on the outer needs of the plants, flowers, trees, humans, and land, protecting them.

This is why just as many good fairy stories are told as bad ones. If a person has negative intentions, the Elemental takes on those characteristics to go forth and bring into form. When a human being is careless and inconsiderate in the Nature Kingdom, these same lovely beings can react with great hostility to get the human's attention. The more a human ignores the signs, the more aggressive the Elementals will get.

The Elementals are also the governing presence of weather patterns working with the Earth itself. They govern the four elements: fire, Earth, water, and air. At times, the Elementals will use weather to clear the discord and toxicity of an area if it becomes too polluted, which is one of the reasons there are hurricanes, storms, lightning, floods, and fires. This is how the Earth heals itself and grows.

The Elementals are in service to this healing and growth. Animals are usually highly alert when major weather changes are going to happen. As part of this kingdom, they know how to read the signs. We also are a part of this kingdom, but most of us have lost contact with the primal connection with nature. Elementals adorn the Nature Kingdom with their healing magic, and can be quite playful with humans when they feel a sense of mutual respect.

The Lemurians are one of the star tribes that still govern an ancient group of Elementals on this planet. Their origin was the continent of Mu, also known as Lemuria. What's left is Hawaii, Fiji, some of the Polynesian Islands, and San Diego, California. Lemurians existed more in their Light Bodies than in denser physical bodies.

They primarily lived on flower essences and were breatharians who live off the prana of air and the vibrational essences of life. Another star tribe that hosts the dolphins is the Sirians from the star Sirius. The Doggon Tribe in Africa was influenced by the Sirians.

The Star Being Elementals and the Angelic Devas work hand in hand as the true stewards of the Earth. The Atlanteans are Planetary Beings that help lay the electrical fields and ley lines of the planet through the use of crystals, gold, gemstones, stone and other minerals. They also work in coordination with these Star Beings and Angels in the co-creation of evolution on Earth. Atlanteans are an example of the Planetary Beings and their use of crystals and other energy systems.

Examples of souls who relate to the Nature Kingdom Tribe of Light are:

- Greta Thunberg *(Swedish youth climate change activist)*
- Steve Irwin *(the Australian crocodile guy)*

- David Attenbourough *(BBC nature programs)*
- Jane Goodall *(Gorilla conservationist)*
- Bear Grylls *(adventurer/ wilderness survival instructor)*
- Deb Haaland *(Native American in house of representative)*
- Autumn Peltier *(Native American Youth fighting for water rights in Canada)*
- Pualani Case aka Auntie Pua *(Hawaiian Activist)*
- Chief Phil Lane *(Native American standing for all Indigenous people and the Earth)*

Meditation

If you feel a connection to this Nature Kingdom Tribe of Light, a great way to connect is sit in nature. Begin breathing into your heart center with long rhythmic breaths. Send white light out the bottom of your feet connecting into the heart of Mother Earth. Focus synchronizing your heartbeat to her heartbeat.

Ask Mother Earth to place you in a "healing vortex chamber of light" with the presence of your soul, the over-lighting Deva of Healing, and the over-lighting Elementals of healing and your Higher Self to bring you into harmonious perfection and healing resonance now. When you can feel the vortex has been established and all the Beings are present, ask to be taken into the Golden Temples of Light within the heart of Gaia. Allow your physical body to rest in this space until you feel complete, 15 to 40 minutes usually. Your soul will travel into this beautiful dimension to seek counsel and guidance. At the completion of your session, send your love, gratitude, and adoration to the heart of the Earth and all the sacred beings that have assisted you. These sessions clear your aura and nervous system, and re-harmonize your life force and meridian system. You will feel balanced and rejuvenated afterwards like you had a full night sleep. If you are traveling, have jet lag, or couldn't get your beauty rest, this will be like a day at the spa.

NATURE KINGDOM GUIDE

Devas: Governed by Archangel Ariel. These are the over-lighting angelic presences for plants, trees, animals, and land masses. An example is Angel Deva of the Jade temple.

Fire Elementals: Governed by Oromasis. The Fire Elementals are known as Salamanders (but not the amphibian we call salamander). They can appear like balls of light or flames and can diminish or expand their energies as needed. Believed to be the most powerful of the Elementals, they are always present in any form of fire. Dragons also dwell within the fire kingdom.

Earth Elementals: Governed by Pan. The Earth Elementals are known as Brownies, Dryads, Durdalis, Earth Spirits, Elves, Hamadryads, Pans, Pixies, Pygmies, Sylvestres, Satyrs, Unicorns, Centaurs, Dwarfs, Leprechauns, Gnomes, Menehune, Giants, Ogres, and Trolls. These beings tend to the gardens, forests, valleys, and all of the soil regions of the Earth, its plants, trees, and animals. They assist in the support of nutrients needed at the root systems and clean up after storms and other messes. They also govern the Mineral Elementals for stones, rocks, crystals, gems, and gold.

Air Elementals: Governed by the Queen of the Fairies Maeve, from the Tuatha de Danann known as the shining ones. In some dimensions, Queen Titania and King Oberon are considered the governing presence. The Air Elements are known as Fairies, Sprites, Pegasus, and Sylphs. These Beings govern the cleaning of the air, coloration of flowers, and all winged creatures such as butterflies, birds, and bats.

Water Elementals: Governed by Neptune. The Water Elementals are known as Undines, Mermaids, Oceanids, Nymphs, Sirens, Limoniades, Naiads, Oreads, Potamides, Water Spirits, and Water Babies. These beings can be seen as shimmering water rays of blues and greens, droplets, sprays, or reflections within waves of the ocean, seas, lakes, rivers, waterfalls, pools, fountains, marshlands, and creeks. They tend to the needs of the plants, coral reefs, and animals within the waters they inhabit. They are cleaning the water.

Remember to do your morning and evening meditation. It's the magic key to activating your Wild Magic!

Morning and Evening Meditation

First, breathe in to your heart for the count of 5 seconds, hold for 5 seconds and breathe out for 10 seconds, while focusing on gratitude for your life, your day, your home, your loved ones, etc.. if you do this 10 times it's about 3 mins to get your head and heart into coherence which opens you up to receive more light, transmissions, downloads, miracles and love or above energy.

Now, focus your awareness 300 feet above your head to a portal of light that connects you to Source Energy.

Command the Cosmic Flow of Pure Love and Light down, in, around and through you. Balancing and harmonizing, cleansing and rejuvenating your entire body and energy. Being it through all your chakras filling them with Pure Love and Light.

Then send this energy to the heart of the new Earth energy. Connect your energy to a place that feels good, peaceful, abundant and supportive for you.

Next, draw this energy back up through the bottoms of your feet, knees, hips and into your heart.

Expand this energy around your body in a 360 degree radius of light. Then send it out all the way around the Planet as a living blessing to all of life.

Open your heart in a circuitry to receive with gratitude Love or Above energy, a synchronicity of miracle, golden opportunities, and really good things coming your way throughout the day and while you sleep raising your vibrational resonance to its highest level possible in all ways in your life.

Hold your hands out in front of you like your holding a basketball. Fill this ball with Pure Love and Light 3x's by saying This is a blessing ball for my day and my life.

Really feel it flooding into this ball of light from your heart center.

I'm filling it with Pure Love and Light, Pure Love and Light, Pure Love and Light!

Purified Source Energy, Purified Source Energy, Purified Source Energy!

Now add Grace and Gratitude. Grace quickens all your blessings and Gratitude opens your heart to receive it.

Say silently or out loud what you want to put into your Blessing Ball:

All problems are instantly resolved with harmonious perfection,

All my needs and desires are met even before I know what I need,

My body is happy and healed, vibrant,

I'm blessing my kids, pets, partner, family, friends, job, Earth, home with Pure Love and Light, I have the perfect partnership that matches my true self energy,

I'm putting in my Blessing Ball kindness, compassion, joy, equanimity in my relationship with myself and others. Forgiveness with any relationship problem.

That as soon as anyone is aware of me or thinks of me they are instantly blessed in Pure Love and Light.

Empowerment, unconditional love, strength, focus, clarity,

My bank accounts are overflowing with hundreds of thousands of dollars, unlimited fulfillment, success, abundance, peace, Love and Above Energy, blessings, miracles.

I'm asking my Tribes of Light, guides, angels and Source Energy to put anything that serves my highest good in my Blessing Ball etc.

Get creative and listen to your heart wisdom.

Next, breathe your Blessing Ball into your heart and radiate it out like a great golden sun all around the Earth to magnetize what you put in your Blessing Ball with Love and Above energy.

Practice:

Always Staying Connected. This will automatically ignite your Soul Blueprint and raise your Vibrational Resonance to your Highest Vibration.

CONCLUSION

It has been a great joy and pleasure being your guide on the journey of your Tribes of Light. Now that you know you have access to these magical worlds and tools of light, remember to use them wisely in the fulfillment of your Soul Blueprint.

Infinite Blessings!

Adrienne Nikki Cobb

ADRIENNE NIKKI COBB

At the age of 15, Adrienne Cobb had a Near Death Experience from a car accident which fully awakened her intuition and ignited her Soul Blueprint. She was touched by The Great Central Sun Angels which changed her life forever. By the age of 20 she was channeling these Angels and connecting people to their own Tribe of Light and Soul Blueprint. Adrienne has done thousands of readings for people internationally. She has written several books and has been interviewed on multiple venues for her intuitive healing abilities. She lives in Portland, Oregon. If you'd like to find out more about what she offers check out her website, podcast, youtube channel at www.mywildmagic.com.